CREATIVE PROBLEM SOLVING:

The Basic Course

by
Scott G. Isaksen
Donald J. Treffinger

Published By Bearly Limited

Copyright © 1985

Bearly Limited
149 York Street
Buffalo, New York 14213

All rights reserved. No part of this publication may be reproduced, stored in retrieval system, or transmitted, in any form or by any means, electronic, mechanical, photocopying, recording, or otherwise, without the prior written permission of the publishers.

Printed in the United States of America
ISBN 0-943456-05-3

Table of Contents

	Dedication & Acknowledgements	vi
	Preface	vii
CHAPTER 1	**Introduction to Creative Problem Solving**	1 - 10
	History: A very abbreviated version	3
	Creative Problem Solving: Its emergence and development	6
	Into the Future-Contemporary Directions in CPS	8
CHAPTER 2	**CPS Overview and Ground Rules**	11 - 22
	Definition of creativity	13
	Importance of CPS	13
	Major stages in the CPS process	15
	The "dynamic balance" in CPS	17
	Some "ground rules" for CPS	17
	"Buckets": What's in a stage?	20
	Using the CPS process efficiently	21
CHAPTER 3	**Mess-Finding: "Getting Started in CPS..."**	23 - 39
	Orientation to the process	25
	Awareness of blocks to creative thinking	27
	Divergence in Mess-Finding	31
	DMF-1: Mess-Finding Matrix	34
	DMF-2: Wallet Checklist	35
	Convergence in Mess-Finding	36
	CMF-1: Mess-Finding Checklist	38
CHAPTER 4	**Data-Finding**	41 - 66
	What is Data-Finding?	43
	Why is Data-Finding important?	45
	Getting started in Data-Finding	46
	Diverging Activities	
	DDF-1: Look and See	47
	DDF-2: Meet the Peanut	48
	DDF-3: Observation Guide	50
	DDF-4: The All-purpose Helper	51
	DDF-5: Stranger than Fiction	53
	DDF-6: The Five W's and an H	55
	DDF-7: Hi-tech Helpers	57
	How much data do you need? When do you have enough data?	58
	Converging Activities	
	CDF-1: D-F Decision Guidelines	59
	CDF-2: Hits, Hot spots, and Relates	60
	CDF-3: Critical Concerns	61
	CDF-4: Must, Need and Like to Know	63
	CDF-5: Data-Finding Matrix	65
	CDF-6: Data-Finding Converging Matrix	66

CHAPTER 5	**Problem-Finding: Structuring the Problem**	67 - 89
	Diverging Activities	
	DPF-1: Listing Ownership and Action Elements	73
	DPF-2: Key Word Variations	75
	DPF-3: The Three Little Pigs	77
	DPF-4: Using the Abstraction Ladder to Broaden or Narrow Problem Statements	78
	DPF-5: Why else? Or how else?	82
	Converging Activities	
	CPF-1: Highlighting	84
	CPF-2: Restatement	88
	CPF-3: Check for Idea-Finding Potential	89

CHAPTER 6	**Idea-Finding**	91 - 114
	Breaking away from habit-bound thinking	94
	Getting in the right mood for Idea-Finding	96
	Ready? Get set. Go!	97
	Diverging Activities	
	DIF-1: What if/Just suppose	99
	DIF-2: Brainstorming Exercise	100
	DIF-3: The Absent-minded Spouse	101
	DIF-4: The Concert	102
	DIF-5: Attribute Listing-Slide Projector	104
	DIF-6: SCAMPER: An Idea Checklist	105
	DIF-7: Forced Relationships	107
	DIF-8: Morphological Analysis: The Writer's Friend	109
	Converging Activities	
	CIF-1: Finding the "Hits"	111
	CIF-2: A-L-U	112
	CIF-3: Hot spots, Relates and Paraphrase	113

CHAPTER 7	**Solution-Finding**	115 - 132
	Use of criteria	117
	Types of criteria	119
	Diverging activities	
	DSF-1: Brainstorming Criteria	121
	DSF-2: Using Criteria Checklists	123
	Converging activities:	
	CC-SF-1: Weighting Criteria	125
	CC-SF-2: Sorting Criteria	127
	CA-SF-1: Using a Grid	129

CHAPTER 8	**Acceptance-Finding**	133 - 149
	Why is Acceptance-Finding important?	135
	Diverging Activities	
	DAF-1: Assisters and Resisters	136
	DAF-2: Planning for Acceptance	138
	DAF-3: Using Criteria to Build Success	139
	DAF-4: Planning for Success	140
	DAF-5: Imaging for Success	142
	Convergence in Acceptance-Finding	143
	Converging activities	
	CAF-1: Implementation Checklist	145

	CAF-2: Checking for Ownership	146
	CAF-3: Planning and Prioritizing First Steps	147
	CAF-4: Recycling Your Plan	148

CHAPTER 9

Putting it All Together — 151 - 194

- Examples of CPS in action — 154
- Sample CPS run-through: Students — 155
- Sample CPS run-through: Dealing with a personal concern — 157
- Sample CPS run-through: Business applications — 159
- A complete CPS run-through of your own — 168
  - Key Questions: Mess-Finding — 169
    - Mess-Finding Worksheet — 170
  - Key-Questions: Data-Finding — 171
    - Data-Finding Worksheet — 172
  - Key Questions: Problem-Finding — 173
    - Problem-Finding Worksheet #1 — 174
    - Problem-Finding Worksheet #2 — 175
    - Problem-Finding Worksheet #3 — 176
  - Key Questions: Idea-Finding — 177
    - Idea-Finding Worksheet #1 — 178
    - Idea-Finding Worksheet #2 (What if/Just suppose) — 179
    - Idea-Finding Worksheet #3 (SCAMPER) — 180
    - Idea-Finding Worksheet #4 (Attribute Listing) — 181
    - Idea-Finding Worksheet #5 (Forced Relationships) — 182
  - Key Questions: Solution-Finding — 183
    - Solution-Finding Worksheet #1 — 184
    - Solution-Finding Worksheet #2 (A-L-U) — 185
    - Solution-Finding Worksheet #3 (PCA) — 186
    - Solution-Finding Worksheet #4 (Matrix) — 187
  - Key Questions: Acceptance-Finding — 188
    - Acceptance-Finding Worksheet — 189
- Contending with time pressure — 190
- Is the entire CPS process always necessary? — 192
- CPS process summary — 192

APPENDIX

Appendix A - CPS Resources — 195 - 203

- To Learn More About CPS — 197

Dedication

In comparison to other "disciplines," creative education is still very young. But the movement has continued to grow in acceptance, stature, scope, and effectiveness throughout the past thirty-five years.

Although there have been many individuals, groups, organizations, and experiences which have had significant impact on our current view of creative problem solving, two stand out in particular for us in importance and value. It is, therefore, to the memory and work of Alex F. Osborn and the colleagueship of Sidney J. Parnes and Ruth B. Noller that we dedicate this book.

Finally, for their encouragement, patience, and support throughout this project, we express our thanks and love for our wives, Marves and Judi.

Acknowledgements

There have been many people who have influenced our thinking and helped us to turn our thinking into a tangible product.

We must acknowledge the rich heritage which provided one steady, historical frame of reference, including our many colleagues and friends at the *Creative Education Foundation* and the *Annual Creative Problem-Solving Institutes*. Specifically, we thank Sid Parnes, Ruth Noller, and Angelo M. Biondi for their leadership and efforts.

Many colleagues and students at the State University College at Buffalo's *Center for Studies in Creativity* and the *Center for Creative Learning* have had input and influence on the content of this book. For their specific contributions to materials, exercises, and ideas we wish to thank Roger Firestien, Peter Lesio, John Moffat, and Susan Stievater. Sue Tannehill and Bob Eberle provided comments and helpful suggestions. In addition, we are grateful to the many students in our creative studies courses and creative learning workshops who have helped us in field-testing and improving the exercises and guidelines we have included.

For the guidance and ideas, we have been most appreciative. The errors that may remain, of course, are ours.

Preface

Creativity has been studied in many different ways. Some writers and researchers sought to understand what makes a person creative, others examined the kind of environment in which creativity thrives, and still others focused on the development of creative products. We are primarily concerned with the creative process, the stages of thinking that are used to meet challenges and overcome obstacles. Of course this process involves people, places, and products as well.

This book is intended to provide you with a basic overview of a systematic process for creative thinking and problem solving. Each stage and phase of this process is described and exercises are provided to build your skills.

We chose a looseleaf format for this book because an open-ended, flexible, and "expandable" format seemed desirable. The creative process is not a static, step-by-step recipe you must follow. Rather, creative problem solving is a system which is natural, dynamic and open. Sometimes you may choose only certain stages or phases. You may also change the order and emphasis of these elements of the process. In short, the main point of the book is not to hand you "our" process, but to provide you knowledge and skills to develop and strengthen your own personal creative problem solving.

This book is based upon our experience and study of more than three decades of research and development on creative problem solving. We have attempted to provide balance between the creative or divergent and the critical or convergent aspects of effective problem solving, and to synthesize current thinking from a wide variety of resources in the field.

Creative problem solving is a method for approaching a challenge or opportunity in a new and relevant way, resulting in successful action. The need for individuals and groups to increase their ability to solve problems creatively is as great today as it was when Harold Harding presented a paper entitled, "The need for a more creative trend in American education," at the Creative Problem-Solving Institute in 1958. In this paper Professor Harding provided three good reasons for concern with creative problem-solving skills.

First, he claimed that creativity was not getting the attention it deserved in high school, college, or graduate and professional school curricula. Second, Harding pointed out that the world of 1958, provided vastly complex problems for which there were not nearly enough ready, willing, and able solvers. Third, he asserted that the broad purpose of American education was training of the mind, by creating environments for scholars and students to work creatively with ideas.

Harding's ideas have stood strong for almost three decades; we believe that they are at least as important today as then. For these reasons, then, we have written this book. We hope that the methods and techniques will be useful to you as you deliberately nurture your own creative potential and guide that of others.

Scott G. Isaksen

Donald J. Treffinger

CHAPTER 1

Introduction to Creative Problem Solving

After studying this chapter, you will be able to:

1. Describe the major historical events in the development of creative problem-solving methods and techniques.
2. Identify specific individuals and organizations contributing to our understanding and application of those methods.
3. Explain major changes that have occurred in our conception of creative learning and problem solving since the 1950s.

Introduction to Creative Problem Solving

The purpose of this book is to provide you with an introduction to *Creative Problem Solving*—a systematic process you can use to become more imaginative and effective in your thinking and action. By learning and applying the simple, easy to use methods and techniques in this book, you will soon notice improvement in your ability to:

1. Recognize opportunities, challenges, and problems;
2. Analyze general situations to identify data that are necessary for effective problem solving;
3. Pose alternative problem interpretations and select appropriate problems or sub-problems;
4. Generate many possible ideas, including new and unusual alternatives;
5. Determine criteria for evaluating alternatives, and apply those criteria to testing possibilities;
6. Analyze promising possibilities to determine possible sources of assistance and resistance to implementation;
7. Formulate and carry out successfully a specific Plan of Action.

> These are the important goals for *Creative Problem Solving: the Basic Course.* Take an extra minute to read through them again. Knowing the goals will help you to guide your own learning efforts!

HISTORY: A VERY ABBREVIATED VERSION

People have been fascinated by the creative process for centuries. It would be possible to demonstrate, for example, that some "intellectuals" in Ancient Greece or Rome pondered the challenge of how we think, use our imagination, and create visions of the future or of solutions to perplexing challenges. For some, of course, creativity has remained a mysterious "gift," or an elusive visit from a Muse, a phenomenon that defies scientific investigation or description.

Modern research in the social and behavioral sciences has demonstrated, however, that the concept of creativity does not have to be mystical or impenetrable, and that our powers of reasoning, analysis, and experimentation can help us attain insights into the nature of creativity and its many faces or expressions.

In the early 1950s, we began to learn that creative thinking involves several cognitive or intellectual abilities that can be defined specifically and even measured among children and adults. In one pioneering effort, J. P. Guilford (1959, 1967, 1977) developed and researched a complex model of human intelligence known as the "Structure-of-Intellect" model (see Figure I-1).

Guilford's research and theory provided insights into the importance of "divergent thinking" (considering many ideas, different kinds of ideas, or unique and unusual ideas), "transformations" (finding ways to change ideas or vary possibilities in systematic ways), and other specific thinking skills in creative behavior.

Another person whose work helped us to understand and assess some fundamental thinking abilities that are related to creativity was E. Paul Torrance (1962, 1963, 1974, 1979). Torrance's definition of creativity emphasized the process of

> *becoming sensitive to problems, deficiencies, gaps in knowledge, missing elements, disharmonies, and so on; identifying the difficulty; searching for solutions, making guesses or formulating hypotheses about the deficiencies; testing and retesting these hypotheses and possibly modifying and retesting them; and finally communicating the results.*

He developed measures to assist us in recognizing the verbal and figural skills of fluency, flexibility, originality, and elaboration that are involved in creative thinking, as well as many materials and resources to help nurture these thinking skills.

Figure I-1. Structure-of-Intellect Model.

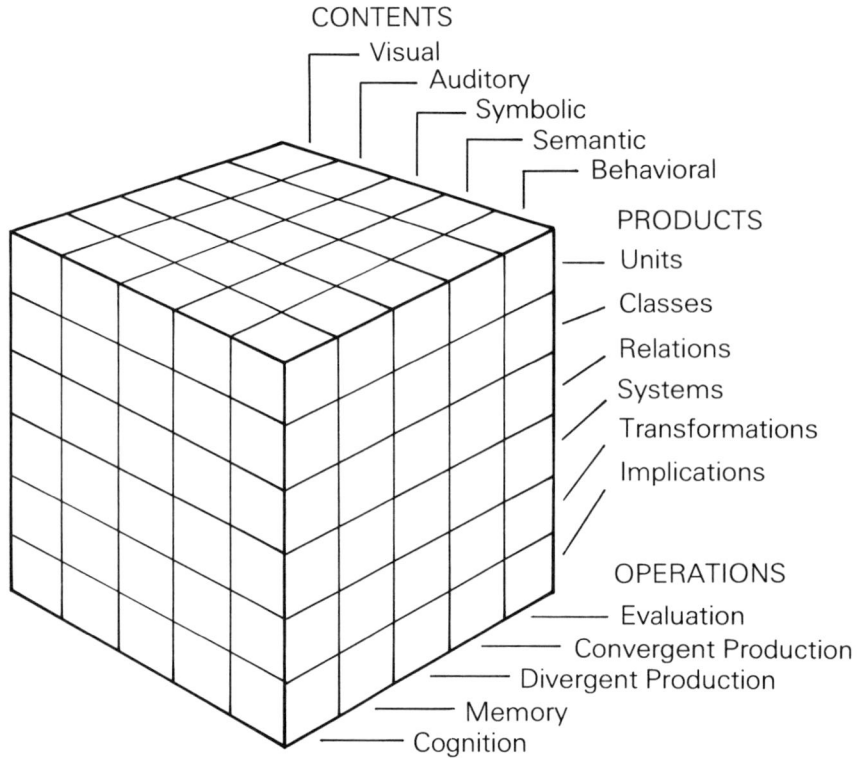

Dr. J. P. Guilford

Dr. E. Paul Torrance

Other views of creativity have been advanced by many writers. Indeed, rather than finding that we are *unable* to develop systematic theories of creativity, there is almost an *overabundance* of such theories. We will not attempt to describe or review them here; brief reviews have been provided by Roweton (1972), Treffinger (1980) and Treffinger, Isaksen, and Firestein (1982, 1983).

Once we were able to clarify our view of some basic thinking abilities involved in creativity, it became much clearer to us that such skills might be learned or improved through instruction. Torrance (1962, 1963) was one of the first educational writers and researchers to attend to this concern. He was instrumental in describing methods and techniques that could be used by teachers or trainers, and in developing prototypes of instructional materials. In the mid-1950s, the efforts of Alex F. Osborn, predicated on the assumption that people could learn to become better creative thinkers, led to the establishment of *The Creative Education Foundation* and its annual *Creative Problem-Solving Institute,* and later to the development of many other programs and publications.

Through the 1960s and early 1970s research on the identification and development of creativity increased rapidly. Torrance (1972) reviewed, for example, more than 140 research studies involving efforts to teach children to think creatively, and Feldhusen and Treffinger (1980) summarized about sixty published resources for promoting creativity and problem solving. Treffinger (1977, 1983) also listed more than 70 kinds of methods, techniques, and educational programs for stimulating creativity. Basadur (1979) and Johansson (1975) showed that programs for stimulating creativity are also widely utilized in many businesses and industries.

The Creative Education Foundation programs grew substantially in numbers, often involving more than 500 people at a single institute, with participants from all over the United States and many foreign countries. The *Journal of Creative Behavior,* founded in 1967, became an established and prestigious resource for those in many disciplines who were interested in creativity. In 1967, Sidney J. Parnes developed the first published version of the instructional program in creative problem solving that was used in the *Creative Problem-Solving Institute* programs, the *Creative Behavior Guidebook.* It was later extensively revised and expanded as the *Guide to Creative Action* (Parnes, Noller, & Biondi, 1977) and the *Creative Actionbook* (Noller, Parnes, & Biondi, 1976).

Many different theories of creativity place varying amounts or degrees of emphasis on the creative process, the personal characteristics or personality of creative individuals, or the dynamics of the social and motivational forces influencing creativity. Some theories stress the themes of personal growth or self-actualization, while others emphasize the historical psychoanalytical views of human behavior. Still others concentrate on the psychedelic, mystical, or non-rational aspects of human creative behavior.

> In the following section, we will explain what we mean by referring to Creative Problem Solving as "cognitive, rational, and semantic." This section looks a little "heavy," but it will explain some of our basic assumptions about people and how they learn.

We have found that the approaches described by psychologists as "cognitive, rational, and semantic" have generally proven both useful and productive in our teaching and research. *Cognitive* refers to our emphasis on creative activity as thoughtful and intellectual in nature. Certainly emotions and personality influence many aspects of everyone's behavior. We do not intend to suggest that your personality or emotions are not related to your creativity and problem solving ability or effectiveness. Rather, we hope to emphasize that you are not merely a "helpless bystander," unable to respond to problems except as your feelings dictate; your ability to think and reason can be used deliberately in creative ways. Similarly, *rational* implies that the activities and skills involved in creative problem solving don't "just happen," or don't occur just as reflexes (like the "knee jerk" or "eye blink" responses). We believe that anyone can deliberately and systematically use the methods and techniques in this program to think and learn more creatively. *Semantic* merely emphasizes that language is a powerful tool available to assist us in our efforts at creative learning and problem solving. This set of tools enables people to generate, organize, compare, combine, replace, store, and evaluate many ideas, including countless possibilities that we have never actually seen, tried, or even experienced in a "first-hand" way. In addition, language makes it possible to develop and use higher-level principles, generalizations, and rules that help in every *new* situation, since they help us generalize and abstract from one experience to another without having to begin "from scratch" each time.

Therefore, as you become involved in learning, practicing and applying the methods and techniques in *Creative Problem Solving: The Basic Course,* you will be learning to use, in a deliberate and orderly way, a powerful set of intellectual tools that can help you become a more imaginative and effective thinker.

QUESTIONS TO CONSIDER

1. Do you agree that it is possible to deliberately become better at thinking creatively and solving problems?

2. Try to make a list of some problems you've solved recently. What are some of the things that helped you to solve those problems? What things made it more difficult?

CREATIVE PROBLEM-SOLVING: ITS EMERGENCE AND DEVELOPMENT

Many ideas in *Creative Problem-Solving: The Basic Course* are derived from a rich heritage of writing, research and practice in the field of creativity and problem-solving. The purpose of this section is to "locate" our work (or establish its context) within that heritage.

Theory and research on creative problem-solving has expanded dramatically during the mid-Twentieth Century, so that all effective problem solvers draw extensively from the principles and methods of many models or approaches. In this sense, most contemporary writers or practitioners must acknowledge that they are indebted to *many* who preceded them. In some ways, most of us are "adapters," building, modifying and using ideas from many sources in original efforts, rather than "innovators," establishing entirely new methods or models. We would be remiss if we did not acknowledge the many and varied mentors whose influence has had an impact on the decisions we have made in this project. These influences have included our reading, study, and often our personal contact with Don MacKinnon, E. Paul Torrance, J. P. Guilford, Calvin Taylor, Bill Gordon, Tony Poze, Stan Gryskiewicz, Synectics Inc., and Kepner-Tregoe, along with many leaders and colleagues at *The Creative Education Foundation's* annual *Creative Problem-Solving Institute.*

We feel, however, a very specific sense of "kinship" or "heritage" with one model; this feeling extends significantly beyond the general "breadth of knowledge" or useful methods and techniques upon which we, like most writers and teachers, have drawn in our work. In *Creative Problem-Solving: The Basic Course,* we have used very explicitly and deliberately a specific approach as the foundation for our work: the widely-known "Osborn-Parnes" Creative Problem-Solving model (Osborn, 1953; Parnes, 1967, 1981; Parnes, Noller & Biondi, 1977; Noller, Parnes, & Biondi, 1976; Noller, 1977; Noller, Treffinger & Houseman, 1979).

In the 1950s Osborn wrote extensively about the importance of imagination and creativity in solving problems. In *Applied Imagination,* Osborn outlined many basic steps to help individuals and groups be more successful in creative thinking. These emphasized techniques and suggestions for fact-finding, idea-finding, and solution-finding (judging ideas). Two basic principles were emphasized: the principle of Deferred Judgment (emphasizing the need to separate the process of *generating* ideas from the process of *evaluating* ideas), and the principle that Quantity Breeds Quality (the more ideas can be gathered, the greater the likelihood of finding some new and useful ideas). With an emphasis on using associative methods (letting one thing lead to another, promoting new and original "connections" of ideas) and deliberate use of creative thinking techniques, Osborn's work became famous for introducing the concept of "Brainstorming" (encouraging a freely-flowing stream of thoughts and ideas, while temporarily withholding all criticism or judgment).

Alex Osborn was a seminal thinker and gifted writer, whose clear and practical explanations of the basic concepts of creative thinking and problem-solving would influence the thinking, teaching, and research of tens of thousands of others over at least a half-century. His *Applied Imagination* (1953) has become one of the most widely read and cited resources in the field, and its concise descriptions and lucid analogies are still germinal for students of creativity in many disciplines.

The power of Osborn's ideas was recognized early by Sidney J. Parnes, who extended those basic concepts into a systematic approach to creative problem solving which could be used effectively in train-

Creative Problem Solving: The Basic Course

Dr. Alex F. Osborn

Dr. Sidney J. Parnes

ing and instruction. Parnes' continuing work on CPS, through teaching, writing, and leadership has helped countless individuals and groups throughout the world develop an appreciation of CPS, confidence in their own creative potential, and skill in using CPS effectively. Through his efforts, along with those of such colleagues as Ruth B. Noller and Angelo M. Biondi, the *Journal of Creative Behavior* and the programs of *The Creative Education Foundation* have had a significant influence on world-wide interest in CPS and its implementation.

Dr. Ruth B. Noller

Angelo M. Biondi

The original emphasis on three stages was expanded into a "five step" Creative Problem-Solving model (Fact-Finding, Problem-Finding, Idea-Finding, Solution-Finding, and Acceptance-Finding). A significant advance was the introduction of a graphic presentation of the five step model.

Figure I-2. Creative Problem-Solving Flowsheet.

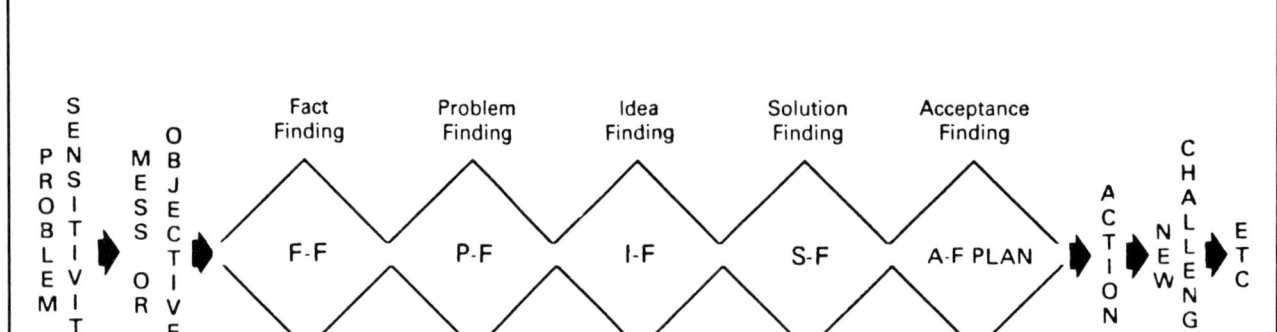

This visual presentation illustrated the interrelationships among the steps and introduced the concept of "balance" between divergent and convergent thinking in CPS. Research on the effectiveness of the CPS model with high school students, college undergraduates, and adults was conducted and published in educational and psychological journals. The *Creative Problem-Solving Institute* expanded, bringing into consideration many additional methods and techniques from a variety of models and theoretical perspectives. The possibility of organizing CPS methods and techniques into systematic instructional programs was expanded.

Although the basic emphases of Osborn's original ideas (Deferred Judgment, Quantity Breeds Quality, Making Associations, Using Techniques Deliberately) were preserved, the actual methods and techniques were expanded considerably, drawing from such additional models as the Creative Analysis approach (Upton, 1961; Upton, Sampson, & Farmer, 1978) and the Synectics approaches (Prince, 1970; Gordon 1966). The major emphasis in CPS moved from a primary focus on brainstorming alone to a "delicate balance" between divergent (many possibilities) and convergent (one response) thinking in the creative problem-solving process. These developments, and the "state of the art" of the CPS approach through this period, were described and summarized effectively by Parnes (1981).

In the 1970's there was also an increasing focus on the *affective* and *interpersonal* aspects of creativity–dimensions often overlooked in theories emphasizing the "cognitive, rational, and semantic" origins of creativity. The development of the CPS approach has been influenced by humanistic models that urge individuals not to overlook the nature of the person within the process; as a result, the methods and techniques involved in CPS have incorporated strategies for dealing with affective (emotional, personal, and inter-personal) needs and responses, through the contributions of such writers and teachers as Eberle and Hall (1975, 1979), Shallcross and Sisk (1982), and others.

INTO THE FUTURE–CONTEMPORARY DIRECTIONS IN CPS

In the late 1970s and the early 1980s, new thrusts have influenced the growth of the Creative Problem-Solving model. We have seen the rapid expansion of technology, and the development of microcomputer technology in particular, with its consequences for our writing, planning, organizing, and forecasting of ideas. These new tools with powerful speed, capacity, and accuracy have expanded the horizons of our thinking. We have become better able to deal with multiple models for processing information, non-linear models of processes, and new directions in information systems. In addition, there have been extensive advances in our understanding of the psychology of individual differences and the science in instruction. We have learned much more than ever before of the many different ways in which individuals and groups behave and learn. We have extended our understanding of the requirements for effective instructional resources, to take into account the varied styles and preferences of learners. Finally, we have become better aware of some new ideas about the characteristics and needs of people in groups (whether in classrooms or places of work) that have guided our investigation of "facilitation" of problem-solving and creative learning.

We (the authors of this book) have been among the benefactors of these advances, as well as of the contributions of our colleagues from the early 1950s to the present. At first, we benefitted indirectly through our own curiosity, reading and study, which brought us into contact with CPS. Subsequently, our involvement has become more direct, initially through our participation in the annual *Creative Problem-Solving Institute* programs, and currently through our professional roles in the *Interdisciplinary Center for Creative Studies* at the State University College at Buffalo. Each of us has "experienced" CPS in different ways: as an undergraduate student in Creative Studies courses, or as a student in the Creative Studies graduate program, as *Institute* participants and leaders, and as faculty or staff in the Creative Studies program. There is both commonality within and diversity among us!

Among the models and methods we have studied and used, the Osborn-Parnes approach has been the strongest and most central in our efforts. This is not true, however, merely as the influence of a "friendly habit" we have nurtured through the years. We have found this model has been very powerful in guiding our research, writing, teaching, and consulting–as well as our own problem-solving. From our first involvement in the early 1960s through the present, the Osborn-Parnes CPS model has provided a sound and productive framework for our efforts. It has also served as a practical and flexible foundation into which we have easily been able to incorporate a variety of techniques and concepts from other approaches. The Osborn-Parnes CPS model has thus continued to provide a practical basis for our investigations and writing. We do not believe that our task in *Creative Problem-Solving: The Basic Course* is to separate or dissociate ourselves from that framework, and so we do not claim to have "invented" a new model, nor to have "replaced" CPS with some striking new approach. (It is, indeed, amusing to us that some of our colleagues appear to be driven to tout and ballyhoo modest refinements of method or technique as if they were major conceptual reformulations of an entire model.)

To be sure however, we also seek to express ideas and to propose methods and techniques that are original and unique in important and specific ways. In that sense, *Creative Problem-Solving: The Basic Course* is not merely a "remake" of earlier publications or materials; nor is it simply an attempt to "update" or expand existing resources or publications. We began our planning of *Creative Problem-Solving: The Basic Course*, within the context of the Osborn-Parnes CPS framework, and we are comfortable in that context. It is also, however, the product of our own imagination, scholarship, and experience with classes, workshops, training seminars, and institutes.

Through the years, many advances and new developments have influenced substantially our day-to-day work with CPS. To say that CPS, as we use it today, is really just the same as it was in 1953, 1967, or 1977, would be the same as saying that a 1984 automobile is really quite the same as a 1964 roadster or that a modern word processor is essentially the same as an electric typewriter. The CPS model with which we began had already become considerably more advanced and sophisticated since the early 50s. Parnes, Noller, and Biondi did more than to reiterate the original ideas of Osborn; they extended and enhanced them substantially. CPS in 1967 and 1977 was as different from its origins as the 1960s automobile from the Model T, or the electric typewriter from the early manual machines.

Our goal is to produce in *Creative Problem-Solving: The Basic Course* a resource that represents a decade of expanding practices and emerging techniques, just as the earlier work of our colleagues extended the original concepts. *Creative Problem-Solving: The Basic Course* is "ours," then, in the sense that we are completely responsible for its contents (and for its shortcomings, too). We hope it will also be a valid and contemporary restatement of the Osborn-Parnes model, from which origins it has been prepared.

Our hope for you, the readers or students who will use these materials, is that in *Creative Problem-Solving: The Basic Course* you will experience the best possible methods and strategies from the well-established, traditional resources of the Osborn-Parnes approach, blended with the most contemporary strategies and resources that we can offer in order to enrich your learning and personal growth as creative problem solvers.

SUGGESTED READINGS

Osborn, A. F. *Applied imagination.* New York: Charles Scribners Sons, 1963 (Third Edition).
Parnes, S. J. *The magic of your mind.* Buffalo, NY: Bearly Limited/Creative Education Foundation, 1981.

REFERENCES CITED

Basadur, M. S. Training in creative problem-solving: effects on deferred judgment and problem finding and solving in an industrial research organization. Unpublished doctoral dissertation, University of Cincinnati, 1979 [Dissertation Abstracts, 40; 5855-B].
Eberle, B. & Hall R. *Affective education guidebook.* Buffalo, NY: D.O.K., 1975.
Eberle, B. & Hall R. *Affective direction.* Buffalo, NY: D.O.K., 1979.
Feldhusen, J. F. & Treffinger, D. J. *Creative thinking and problem-solving in gifted education.* Dubuque, IA: Kendall-Hunt, 1980.
Gordon, W. J. J. *Synectics.* NYC: Harper, 1961.
Guilford, J. P. Three faces of intellect. *American Psychologist,* 1959, *14,* 469-479.
Guilford, J. P. *The nature of human intelligence.* NYC: McGraw-Hill, 1967.
Guilford, J. P. *Way beyond the IQ.* Buffalo, NY: Creative Education Foundation, 1977.
Johansson, B. *Creativity and creative problem-solving courses in United States industry.* Greensboro, NC: Center for Creative Leadership, 1975.
Kepner, C. & Tregoe, B. *The new rational manager.* Princeton, NJ: Kepner-Tregoe, 1982.
Noller, R. B. *Scratching the surface of creative problem-solving.* Buffalo, NY: D.O.K., 1977.
Noller, R. B., Parnes, S. J. & Biondi, A. M. (eds.). *Creative actionbook.* NYC: Charles Scribners Sons, 1976.
Noller, R. B., Treffinger, D. J. & Houseman, E. D. *It's a gas to be gifted: CPS for the gifted and talented.* Buffalo, NY: D.O.K., 1979.
Osborn, A. F. *Applied imagination.* NYC: Charles Scribners Sons, 1953.
Parnes, S. J. *Creative behavior guidebook.* NYC: Charles Scribners Sons, 1967.
Parnes, S. J. *The magic of your mind.* Buffalo, NY: Bearly Limited, 1981.
Parnes, S. J., Noller, R. B. & Biondi, A. M. (eds.). *Guide to creative action.* NYC: Charles Scribners Sons, 1977.
Prince, G. M. *The practice of creativity.* NYC: Harper & Row, 1970.
Roweton, W. *Creativity: a review of theory and research.* Buffalo, NY: Creative Education Foundation, 1972.
Shallcross, D. & Sisk, D. *The growing person.* Englewood Cliffs, NJ: Prentice-Hall, 1982.
Torrance, E. P. *Guiding creative talent.* Englewood Cliffs, NJ: Prentice-Hall, 1962.
Torrance, E. P. *Education and the creative potential.* Minneapolis, MN: University of Minnesota Press, 1963.
Torrance, E. P. Can we teach children to think creatively? *Journal of Creative Behavior,* 1972, *6,* 114-143.
Torrance, E. P. *Torrance tests of creative thinking.* Lexington, MA: Ginn/Xerox, 1974.
Torrance, E. P. *The search for satori and creativity.* Buffalo, NY: Creative Education Foundation, 1979.
Treffinger, D. J. Methods, techniques, and educational programs for stimulating creativity. In Parnes, S. J., Noller, R. B. & Biondi, A. M. (eds.), *Guide to creative action.* NYC: Charles Scribners Sons, 1977.
Treffinger, D. J. *Encouraging creative learning for the gifted and talented.* Ventura, CA: Ventura County Supt. of Schools, LTI Publications, 1980.
Treffinger, D. J. Methods, techniques, and educational programs for stimulating creativity: 1982 revision. In Tannenbaum, A. J., *Gifted children: psychological and educational perspectives.* NYC: Macmillan, 1983, 467-504.
Treffinger, D. J., Isaksen, S. G. & Firestien, R. L. *Handbook of creative learning.* Honeoye, NY: Center for Creative Learning, 1982.
Treffinger, D. J., Isaksen, S. G. & Firestien, R. L. Theoretical perspectives on creative learning and its facilitation: an overview. *Journal of Creative Behavior,* 1983, *17 (1),* 9-17.
Upton, A. *Design for thinking.* Palo Alto, CA: Pacific Books, 1961.
Upton, A., Sampson, R. W. & Farmer, A. D. *Creative analysis.* NYC: Dutton, 1978.

CHAPTER

CPS Overview and Ground Rules

After studying this chapter, you will be able to:

1. Define creativity and explain the six stages of creative problem solving.
2. Identify and explain six basic ground rules for divergent and convergent thinking.
3. Recognize and identify examples of CPS stages.

CPS Overview and Ground Rules

In this chapter, our major goal is to introduce the Creative Problem-Solving process. (From now on we will simply use the acronym "CPS," instead of writing out "Creative Problem Solving" in full each time.) In this chapter, we intend to provide only a general overview of what CPS is all about, so don't be concerned if you feel uncertain about your grasp of the process. As we proceed through *Creative Problem Solving: The Basic Course,* we will take a detailed look at all the steps and techniques that are "highlighted" in this chapter.

DEFINITION OF "CREATIVITY"

There are many definitions of creativity. For our purposes, however, we will define creativity in this way:
CREATIVITY is Making and Communicating meaningful new connections–
- to help us think of many possibilities;
- to help us think and experience in varied ways and using different points of view;
- to help us think of new and unusual possibilities;
- to guide us in generating and selecting alternatives.

THE IMPORTANCE OF CPS

There are many reasons for the importance of CPS; just think about
- the opportunities you'd like to meet.
- the wishes, hopes, dreams, and aspirations you hold.
- the problems and challenges in your life.

It won't help much merely to wait for someone else to take care of these challenges for you! Children won't always have their teachers or parents around, waiting to help them solve their problems or to show them how to do that, and adults can't just sit back and hope that problems will vanish. To be effective in meeting the many challenges of our everyday personal and professional lives, everyone can benefit from knowing and using some simple, practical strategies for creative problem-solving.

CPS is important because it helps us tackle problems on our own in a practical and effective manner.

If you give a man a fish, he will have a meal.
If you teach him to fish, he will have a living.

In addition, however, we all need to know CPS methods and techniques for other reasons. Because of the rapid expansion of knowledge and information in our world, it is no longer possible to assume confidently that the "facts" learned in school or on the job provide all the knowledge necessary to deal successfully with new situations. In fact, the "lifetime" of knowledge is getting shorter and shorter, with rapid advances and improved communications in almost every discipline quickly making obsolete things we thought we "knew" only a short time before. Everyone needs to know how to find and use information and how to deal with constantly changing situations. We must be able to deal effectively with many situations that we've never encountered before, and for which our prior learning or experience has not prepared us: the unexpected, the unpredicted, the unanticipated, or the newly-developed challenge. For these situations, we need the thinking skills or "tools" provided by CPS.

> **CPS helps us to deal effectively with future problems and challenges that we can't even anticipate at the present time!**

CPS is also important because it provides opportunities to learn in our most preferred ways, and it offers learning opportunities that can have a powerful impact on our life. Our experience with many groups—from elementary school children to college students to teachers and professors to business people, scientists and engineers—has revealed that contacts with creative learning and CPS frequently provide individuals with their most memorable and important learning experiences. (Many of us have known, for example, some individuals who, well into adulthood, became intensely involved in some form of creative learning—perhaps as a hobby—and then found that it became an all-consuming "passion" that quickly became a new career for them. In addition, many people who have learned to use CPS have found new sources of energy, challenge, and stimulation in their own life and work.

> **Creative learning and CPS can have a very positive and powerful impact on our lives and careers.**

A person's involvement in CPS can also bring new sources of satisfaction and reward in personal growth, professional accomplishments, and relations with other people. CPS can be a "tool" to help people to discover and use new talents, to function more effectively, to immerse themselves in meaningful projects, and to share their ideas and accomplishments with others. This does *not* mean that creative endeavors involving CPS will be "easy," despite the unfortunate tendency of many people to equate satisfaction and ease. In fact, many people report that they *work very hard* to use CPS–but they promptly add that the benefits and results more than adequately justify their efforts.

> **CPS is not always easy, but it does lead to great satisfaction and reward.**

Finally, we have observed that people who learn to use CPS experience a strong sense of "balance" or "synthesis" in intellectual effort that is important and beneficial for them. They learn that *creative* and *critical* thinking, imagination and judgment, can work together productively–that these are not mutually exclusive or "conflicting" processes. In addition, through CPS, we learn to use our critical or judgmental facilities in new and constructive ways, by learning how to find promising ideas and "building them up," rather than merely using critical thinking to attack, eliminate, or "tear down" ideas.

We are viewing critical thinking in a more productive manner. Critical and creative thinking are mutually important aspects of effective problem solving. For us,

CRITICAL THINKING is analyzing and developing possibilities to:
- compare and contrast many ideas;
- improve and refine promising alternatives;
- screen, select, and support ideas;
- make effective decisions and judgments; and
- provide a sound foundation for effective action.

> CPS helps us find constructive and affirmative ways to use our creative *and* critical thinking abilities.

MAJOR "STAGES" IN THE CPS PROCESS

In CPS, there are six major components or stages. These are:

- Mess-Finding
- Data-Finding
- Problem-Finding
- Idea-Finding
- Solution-Finding
- Acceptance-Finding

Let's begin by taking a closer look at each of these six stages. Each phase will be described briefly. A graphic summary of the stages is given in Figure II-1 on the next page.

- **Mess-Finding.** The first stage, called Mess-Finding, involves probing our interests, experiences, and concerns to consider a number of general topics which might serve as possibilities or starting-points for CPS. Sometimes, of course, we know immediately that there's a certain situation, or "mess" that demands our attention and response. But at other times (and especially when learning the CPS method) we will need to know how to deliberately search for a "mess" on which to work.

In addition, Mess-Finding involves knowing how to choose, prioritize, or select one mess to investigate from a large number of alternatives. You'll learn several techniques for finding and selecting "messes" in *Chapter Three*.

- **Data-Finding.** The second stage of the process, Data-Finding, helps you begin working on your Mess. In this stage, you will increase your awareness of the Mess by "taking stock:" gathering all available information, knowledge, facts, feelings, thoughts, opinions, or questions about the Mess. You're taking an inventory of everything you know, need, or want to know, to help better understand the actual size and shape of the Mess. Data-Finding helps you analyze and clarify the situation, to sort out or analyze and clarify the Mess. It helps in beginning to identify potential problems requiring your effort and attention. In the convergent phase of Data-Finding, you will make decisions about which data seem to have special significance or importance, or which data require special consideration in preparation for formulating problem statements. You will learn specific methods and techniques for Data-Finding in *Chapter Four*.

- **Problem-Finding.** In Problem-Finding, your task is to consider many possible questions, or "problem statements", about which you want to gather ideas. Putting aside the common assumption that you "already know what the problem is," you'll stretch your imagination to consider a number of possible statements of problems or sub-problems. You will try to look at the data you considered most important from the Data-Finding stage to determine what problem statements might be suggested. (There are *several* problem statements that might be suggested by the data in almost every problem we've ever seen!) You will seek to find problem statements that literally invite you to think of many new and interesting ideas. In the converging phase of Problem-Finding, you'll seek a problem statement, or a combination of problem statements that seems best to fit the most important aspects of the situation, and that you believe does the best job of expressing the "heart" of the situation. You will learn a number of specific techniques in *Chapter Five* to help you with Problem-Finding.

- **Idea-Finding.** The stage of the CPS process called Idea-Finding involves searching for many possible responses or ideas for the question or problem statement selected in Problem-Finding. In Idea-Finding, your goal is to find as many ideas or alternatives as possible, using a wide variety of methods and techniques to help you create many, varied, and original possibilities. The more ideas you can produce, the greater the likelihood that some will represent promising solutions to the problem. In the converging

Figure II-1.

CREATIVE PROBLEM SOLVING PROCESS

DIVERGENT PHASE	PROBLEM SENSITIVITY	CONVERGENT PHASE
Experiences, roles and situations are searched for messes... openness to experience; exploring opportunities.	MESS FINDING (diverge / converge)	Challenge is accepted and systematic efforts undertaken to respond to it.
Data are gathered; the situation is examined from many different viewpoints; information, impressions, feelings, etc. are collected.	DATA FINDING	Most important data are identified and analyzed.
Many possible statements of problems and sub-problems are generated.	PROBLEM FINDING	A working problem statement is chosen.
Many alternatives and possibilities for responding to the problem statement are developed and listed.	IDEA FINDING	Ideas that seem most promising or interesting are selected.
Many possible criteria are formulated for reviewing and evaluating ideas.	SOLUTION FINDING	Several important criteria are selected to evaluate ideas. Criteria are used to evaluate, strengthen, and refine ideas.
Possible sources of assistance and resistance are considered; potential implementation steps are identified.	ACCEPTANCE FINDING	Most promising solutions are focused and prepared for action; Specific plans are formulated to implement solution.

NEW CHALLENGES

phase of Idea-Finding, you'll decide which ideas seem most promising or appealing and thus deserve further analysis and examination. Idea-Finding methods will be explained in *Chapter Six*. In Solution-Finding, you will use specific criteria to analyze your most promising ideas.

- **Solution-Finding.** The first step in Solution-Finding is to consider many possible criteria for evaluating your most promising ideas. What "standards" will the ideas need to meet to determine their strengths and weaknesses? What criteria will help you determine which ideas are truly promising, and where lie their greatest advantages or limitations? Then, selecting the criteria you decide are the most important or necessary to consider, you will analyze your promising ideas carefully and systematically. The result of this stage will be to determine which idea or ideas–(there may be several really promising ones!–) offer the greatest potential for solving the problem. *Chapter Seven* will provide many specific Solution-Finding methods.

- **Acceptance-Finding.** In the Acceptance-Finding stage, you will be concerned with taking those promising problem-solving possibilities and considering the specific elements that will promote successful implementation. You don't want to have some great solutions that aren't put to use! You'll consider many aspects of action that will either *assist* or *resist* your efforts to solve the problem. You'll consider many possible obstacles, objections, or difficulties which could get in the way, and many possible sources of support and encouragement. Then, in the convergent phase, you'll decide what implementation steps are most important and develop a specific, step-by-step Plan of Action. Methods and techniques for successful Acceptance-Finding are provided in *Chapter Eight*.

THE "DYNAMIC BALANCE" IN CPS

As you looked at Figure II-1, you probably noticed that each of the six stages of CPS was enclosed in a diamond-shaped box. Perhaps you thought those diamonds were just a little fancy art work to make the figure look more attractive. On the contrary, however, they were included deliberately, because they represent something very important to remember about CPS. They remind us that each stage of the process begins with efforts to search, to stretch our thinking, and to consider many possibilities. We refer to this as the "divergent" (going in many directions) aspect of CPS. The diverging is followed in each stage by efforts to screen, select, or choose the most important or promising possibilities. This is referred to as the "convergent" (closing in on one or a few items) aspect of CPS.

Keeping this in mind helps to avoid a common error in many peoples' ideas about creativity. Contrary to some popular misunderstandings, creativity is *not* merely rattling off one crazy idea after another, letting everything go wild, without ever judging or evaluating. It is important to be able to make good choices and decisions about ideas. In CPS, we learn to use effective methods for generating *and* evaluating ideas, and we try to accomplish a reasonable balance between "diverging" and "converging." We talk about this as the "dynamic balance" that makes CPS powerful and productive.

SOME "GROUND RULES" FOR CPS

Some basic "ground rules" will help you to be more effective in your thinking during each of the six CPS stages. Some of these are basic principles that will make the divergent thinking easier and more productive, while others will be more helpful during the convergent thinking phases. We will remind you frequently about these ground rules in the chapters dealing with the six CPS stages. They are really fundamental principles to make it easier for you to remember and use all the specific "tools" (methods and techniques) that will be presented in each chapter. You should try to become so familiar with these basic ground rules that they will become "second nature" to you during CPS.

Divergent Ground Rules

There are six ground rules for the divergent aspects of each stage. These principles will assist you in searching for a truly extensive collection of ideas!

1. *DEFER JUDGMENT.* This is the most fundamental of all the ground rules. "Defer judgment" reminds us that it is important to keep your mind open to all possibilities, and to avoid using evaluation prematurely to "squelch" or inhibit the free flow of ideas. In any

CPS endeavor, *ideas* are the heart of the process, so we want to avoid any habits or behavior which could cause us to overlook or disregard possibilities during our initial searching.

An analogy used by Alex Osborn is very helpful. Consider the gas and brake pedals on a car. They're both essential controls and a driver must use them both. However, in all but a few very unusual circumstances, you don't use them both simultaneously. It wouldn't be very helpful to depress *both* the accelerator *and* the brake pedal, but it *is* important to know how and when to use each one. Searching for ideas works much the same way: there's a time to generate possibilities, and a time to evaluate them, but both processes are more effective when used separately. "Defer judgment" does not mean that ideas won't *ever* be evaluated ("defer" is not the same as "eliminate"). It does mean that when we are attempting to generate many possibilities, we have to remember not to hold back any ideas. You should not be too quick to say, "No, that won't work!" or "That's a dumb idea!"–to yourself or to others, because premature criticism of ideas can stifle thinking and cause stress or lack of confidence among group members. In addition, deferring judgment also involves not being too quick to praise an idea. Don't get trapped by letting yourself too easily think or say, "Oh! Wow! That's *it*! I don't need any more ideas now."

2. *LOOK FOR LOTS OF IDEAS.* During the divergent phase in each CPS stage, you're trying to find as many ideas as possible. Don't worry about their quality–that will be your concern in the converging phases and during Solution-Finding and Acceptance-Finding. Usually, this will help you to make a deliberate effort to search for many possibilities. Many of your ideas may be very common or obvious, but some might be useful or can be modified to create new ideas that haven't occurred to you before. In addition, writing down all those ideas helps you get them off your mind, "clearing up some space," as it were, for fresh, new possibilities. Not infrequently, "Quantity breeds quality."

3. *ACCEPT ALL IDEAS.* Don't be afraid to be playful in your thinking during the divergent phase. Entertain *every* idea that comes to mind, no matter how strange, wild, or silly it may seem at first glance. If you keep a record of a wild or silly idea, you may later discover it's really fascinating, and you can find ways to "tame it down" or modify it to put it to use. But if you had simply dismissed or disregarded it, the idea would be lost. In addition, ideas that might appear "strange," "silly" or even "crazy" to some people or at some times, have later provided the foundation for very original and powerful ideas for others.

4. *MAKE YOURSELF "STRETCH."* Many people tend to be rather lazy in their thinking. They're willing to spend a few minutes trying to think of possibilities, get a few ideas, and then say, "Well that's about all I can think of." But effective creative problem-solving requires *extended* effort. We need to keep at it, searching for ideas that don't just pop into mind right away. Some people have successfully used methods of stimulating creativity that "push" participants to keep thinking for many hours at a time. New and original ideas often occurred when group members were nearing their limits–approaching a state of physical or mental exhaustion. Calling on all your senses can enrich the thinking that you're doing. It's often helpful to "stretch" your thinking by deliberately providing fresh "input" through the senses (for example, by looking around at your environment, scanning pictures or a newspaper, listening to music, tasting or smelling something, touching something, or even doing some exercise).

5. *TAKE TIME TO LET IDEAS "SIMMER."* If you're really trying to gather many possibilities, it can be helpful to put the problem aside for awhile after you've started gathering some ideas and before you start to converge or to move to the next stage. This allows you to put the problem in the back of your mind, to stimulate the phenomenon known as "incubation." Although you may believe you've put the problem aside, you may find that you've continued to mull it over, without being explicitly aware of doing it, and some new ideas may seem to occur very suddenly or in the middle of some other activity. For that reason,

it's especially helpful to carry what we call an "Idea System," such as a small pocket notebook, for jotting down ideas that may come to mind at unusual or unexpected times.

6. *SEEK COMBINATIONS–BE A "HITCH-HIKER."* Many people consider the ability to make "new connections" to be the very essence of the creative process. It's certainly true that it is very helpful in CPS to be able to draw together pieces from several different ideas to form new and unusual possibilities. Your efforts to think divergently during each CPS stage will be enhanced if you remain alert to opportunities to combine various ideas from yourself or others to form new possibilities that are even more promising than any of the parts that went into them. We speak of this as "hitch-hiking" one idea with another.

Convergent Ground Rules

There are also some basic principles to help you become more efficient and effective during the converging phase of each of the six CPS stages:

1. *BE DELIBERATE.* The convergent phase of each stage calls for you to make choices and decisions. This effort is often greatly facilitated by deliberate, planful or systematic thinking. Logical, critical thinking is really part of good CPS. Your decisions and Plan of Action will probably be better, and more likely to be successful, if you've used a careful, well-planned approach to decision-making at each stage. Being deliberate means developing a plan and using logic and good sense.

2. *BE EXPLICIT.* Difficulty or controversy in problem-solving or implementation often occurs when there are some hidden agendas or criteria that aren't known to everyone. Your efforts to converge will be more successful and more readily communicated and discussed with others when you are very clear, honest and specific about the basis used for evaluating possibilities and ideas. Being explicit means getting things out in the open, for anyone to know, see, or evaluate.

3. *AVOID PREMATURE CLOSURE.* Before you reach a decision, be sure you have given many possibilities fair consideration. It is sometimes easy to look over a list of ideas and to be too content to settle for the ones that look most "comfortable" or familiar while overlooking unique, original, or unusual ideas which might be very promising if examined closely. (When people do this, they often complain, "Well I used CPS, but I didn't come up with anything very new or different." They didn't *let* themselves consider anything very new or different!) Take some extra time to "play" with the unusual ideas in any list before reaching a decision, to remain alert for promising but unusual opportunities.

4. *TAKE THE RISK TO LOOK AT DIFFICULT ISSUES OR "SNEAKY SPOTS."* Don't assume that some of those really difficult or unpleasant matters in many problems will simply go away if you ignore them. In problem-solving as in health, such things *don't* go away, and can often be addressed more successfully by considering them openly and as early as possible. You should also make a deliberate effort to anticipate some problems or difficulties that might not be obvious, but which *will* influence your planning and decisions about ideas. As you look at the list of ideas, are there any trouble spots or areas of concern that you hadn't thought about before? Thinking about this as you proceed will help you avoid being devastated by those concerns later on (what we call getting "submarined" when you're preparing to implement some ideas). Don't "kid yourself" about these concerns, but deal with them in a direct and realistic way.

5. *DEVELOP A SENSE OF "AFFIRMATIVE JUDGMENT."* Don't approach the task of converging, or making choices and decisions about a list, simply as a matter of "idea-slaughtering." You're not trying to eliminate ideas or possibilities. Rather, it will be helpful to train yourself to look for strengths or positive aspects of ideas. What are some things that appeal to you about the possibilities you've created? What intriguing new thoughts

are suggested by some of your unusual ideas? What's *good* about some of the ideas? *Affirmative* judgment reminds us that evaluation and decision-making are constructive processes, not just destructive criticism.

6. *KEEP YOUR EYES ON YOUR OBJECTIVES.* While attempting to converge or to select the most important or promising possibilities from your list, remember the general goals and objectives you're trying to achieve using CPS. Don't get so caught up in the process of producing or evaluating ideas that you stray from the concerns that are really most important to you.

Figure II-2.

"BUCKETS": WHAT'S IN A STAGE?

As you proceed through each of the following chapters, you will find that, for each stage of the CPS process, several methods and techniques will be provided for you to use in your problem-solving efforts. You will not need every method you've learned for each stage whenever you work on a problem, however. We'd like you to think about each of the six stages as if it were a large container, or "bucket", capable of holding lots of ideas, methods, or techniques. When you begin to work on a certain stage of CPS in your problem-solving, look into the "bucket," and ask, "What's in this bucket that will help me with this problem?" Try the methods that seem most promising; if they do the job–fine! If not, look back into the "bucket" and see what else is there that might be helpful.

Figure II-3.

USING THE CPS PROCESS EFFICIENTLY

Just as you will sometimes need and use only some methods or "tools" in each "bucket," your use of all six stages of the CPS process may also vary, depending upon the circumstances or situation, the time, the resources available, and your interest or ability. There will certainly be some situations in which you will find it helpful to use *all* the CPS stages. At other times, however, you may find it will be necessary only to use *some* of the stages. We don't *always* start at the beginning or go through every stage of the process. There may be some situations in which you are already "one hundred percent certain" of your problem definition, or of the solution that best fits the problem. In such cases, you may need only to put your solution into Action, so you can begin with an implementation stage (which we call "Acceptance-Finding"). At other times, you might have the same degree of certainty about the problem definition, but recognize that several options exist from which to choose. In this case, you would do well to examine those options by using specific criteria (a decision-making stage called "Solution-Finding"). In yet other situations, you may be absolutely certain about the problem definition, but really need to generate some options; in this case, perhaps a few minutes of brainstorming with friends would suffice (an idea-generating stage, which we call "Idea-Finding"). In each of these cases, you might not be using the *entire* CPS process. You might use certain methods and techniques from various stages, while a very systematic, structured use of *all* the stages might be unnecessary. Creative thinking can be applied to virtually *any* problem situation; a complete, systematic application of the CPS process will help you greatly when you need to be innovative–in any situation in which you're not "100% Certain" about what the problem is.

But! A Word of Caution!

We've met a few people who are "100% Certain" about *all* their problems and solutions! They have no need for a creative problem-solving process, they say, because all their problems are already solved. This can be one of the most pervasive blocks to creative thinking. Lack of problem sensitivity allows these individuals to persist in patterns of thinking and behaving that are often rigid, habit-bound, and unsuccessful. Somehow, we're more comfortable with positions that allow greater "margins" for openness to problem redefinition. Being aware that your *current* definition of a problem is not the only possible definition is an important part of most approaches to creative problem-solving. This awareness enables you to be more deliberate in formulating ideas and selecting among alternatives, rather than pretending that all the options are known. On the basis of considerable research (e.g., Maier, 1970; Torrance, 1979; Guilford, 1977; MacKinnon, 1978) we hold that willingness to consider alternatives, to take some risk, to venture into uncertain territory, and to tolerate some ambiguity in problem-solving are necessary and important ingredients of effective thinking. Don't be too quick to assume that there's "no problem."

In *Chapter Three* on Mess-Finding, you will learn about methods and techniques to help you decide how to make good decisions about using the six CPS stages.

REFERENCES CITED

Guilford, J. P. *Way beyond the I. Q.* Buffalo, NY: Bearly Limited/Creative Education Foundation, 1977.

MacKinnon, D. W. *In search of human effectiveness: Identifying and developing creativity.* Buffalo, NY: Bearly Limited/Creative Education Foundation, 1978.

Maier, N. R. *Problem-solving and creativity in individuals and groups.* Belmont, CA: Brooks-Cole, 1970.

Torrance, E. P. *The search for Satori and creativity.* Buffalo, NY: Bearly Limited/Creative Education Foundation, 1979.

CHAPTER 3

Mess-Finding: "Getting Started in CPS..."

> **Mess-Finding Stage**
>
> Experiences, roles and situations are searched for challenges and concerns. A Mess is accepted and systematic efforts are undertaken to respond to it.

After studying this chapter, you will be able to:

1. Describe many specific situations or goals ("Messes") that can be addressed using CPS.
2. Identify and explain your own orientation toward the CPS process.
3. Describe the role of personal or learning styles in approaching problem-solving situations.
4. Describe and give examples of personal, situational and problem-solving blocks that may inhibit creative problem-solving efforts.
5. Identify several aspects of an atmosphere conducive to creative growth.
6. Identify the meaning of "outcomes" and "obstacles" in CPS and give examples of each in Mess-Finding.
7. Describe three important guidelines for effective Mess-statements and use those guidelines in formulating your own Messes for problem solving.
8. Use the Mess-Finding Matrix to analyze various personal Messes.
9. Describe and explain three specific criteria for Ownership for a Mess.
10. Describe and explain four specific criteria for evaluating your Outlook toward a Mess.
11. Evaluate and select Messes by applying specific criteria for ownership and outlook to your own Messes.
12. Use a Mess-Finding Checklist to make decisions regarding your choice of Messes for problem solving.

Mess-Finding: "Getting Started in CPS..."

The first step in the Creative Problem-Solving process is "Mess-Finding." During this stage you are structuring your problem-solving efforts to identify and accept a challenge.

Before submitting a challenge to deliberate problem-solving efforts, it is essential to put off the natural tendency to "leap for a solution." A more productive way to get started involves "massaging" the situation: examining it and uncovering its elements. This permits you to choose the most promising avenues to investigate. Mess-Finding sets the scope for your efforts; it is the stage of CPS during which deliberate effort is extended to identify the significant elements or components of the challenge you are attempting to meet. It is helpful to think about a "Mess" because it reminds you that the initial problem with which you are dealing is very broad, perhaps even "fuzzy" or poorly defined. You also need to resist the temptation to define the solution prematurely.

Your Mess-Finding efforts will help you to untangle complicated situations so you can direct your problem-solving efforts where you really want them. Real problem situations are rarely encountered in a clear, neatly-stated precise form; some time and energy must be spent to get them ready to solve.

As you have already read in *Chapter Two,* the stages of the CPS process alternate between divergent and convergent thinking. As with the other stages of CPS, Mess-Finding starts with divergent thinking. Your problem sensitivity is heightened by searching for messes from your personal or professional experiences and roles, and exploring the situations that are on your mind day in and day out. This is "divergent" because each of us has many such experiences, wishes, or concerns that might be on our mind at any time. This divergent aspect of Mess-Finding is closely aligned with the concept of "openness to experience."

As MacKinnon (1978) indicated:

> *Creative persons are especially open to experience, both of the inner self and of the outer world . . . they are open to and receptive of experience and seeking to know as much as possible about life. (pg. 129)*

ORIENTATION TO THE PROCESS

One area you need to be aware of during CPS is your orientation toward the process of problem solving. What are your preferred patterns of dealing with various situations? What are your problem-solving strengths? Your interests? The answers to these questions should guide you in deciding your general direction for problem-solving efforts.

There have been many approaches to studying thinking styles, learning styles, and personality types. Many include the use of a variety of assessment devices (formal and informal) to gather information about your style or preferences in relation to the problem-solving process. You can gain an understanding of how you typically approach problem solving by using these instruments.

Such instruments typically offer a number of categories or types. For example, the Myers-Briggs Type Indicator (Myers, 1980) includes four general categories of preferences derived from the work of Carl Gustav Jung. The Myers-Briggs Type Indicator (which we will call the MBTI) is concerned with differences in people that result from the way they like to find things out and the way they like to make decisions. In additiion, the instrument examines your preferences regarding extraversion and introversion as well as the use of perception and judgment in dealing with the world.

The first dimension of the MBTI describes whether you prefer the outer world of people and things or the inner world of ideas and concepts. This is referred to as *extraversion* or *introversion.* If you know how you stand in this area, you can be more interested and comfortable when you work on challenges and opportunities which relate to your preference for working with others or things, or working quietly inside your head. The MBTI also examines opposing ways of "finding out" including *sensing* and *intuition.* Knowledge of these dimensions tells about your preference for using your senses as opposed to personal insights in gathering information.

Another dimension deals with opposite ways of deciding. According to the MBTI, one way to decide is through *thinking*. Thinking considers and predicts the logical results of actions you take. The decision is made on the basis of an impersonal examination of causes and effects. The other way to decide is through *feeling*. Feeling considers anything of importance to you, without requiring that it be logical. The decision is made on the basis of personal values.

Knowledge of this dimension will be helpful during problem-solving by allowing you to know the kind of deciding you naturally prefer. By matching, massaging and blending the messes you deal with to capitalize on the kind of deciding that comes naturally, your decisions will be better and will be made with more confidence.

The final area assessed by the MBTI is your preference to face the outer world with an attitude that is judging or perceptive. If you prefer *judging*, you rely mainly on thinking and feeling and live in a planned, decided, orderly way. You want to regulate life and control it. If you prefer *perceiving*, you depend mostly on sensing or intuition to deal with the outer world, and live in a flexible, spontaneous way, wanting to understand life and adapt to it.

These then are the four preferences:

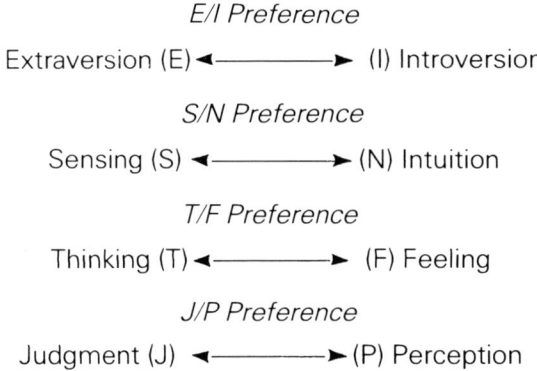

Your type is determined by your own combination of preferences. For ease of comparing your type with others, types are described by the four letters showing your preferences (e.g., INTJ means Introversion-Intuition-Thinking-Judgment). INTJ people are original, and in fields that appeal to them, they are skillful at organizing tasks and carrying them through. They tend to be skeptical, critical, independent, determined, and sometimes stubborn. It is important for them to learn when to "yield" on less important points in order to "win" on more critical issues. Similar descriptions of each type, with additional information about the implications for thinking and behavior are provided by the manual.

As is true for many other instruments designed to provide a quick evaluation of your style or type, several things should be considered when using the MBTI. Your results probably do not provide a complete view of *all* your important personality or thinking styles. Also, many dimensions included on this type of instrument may not really be "either/or" in nature. That is, they do not suggest that you *only* use a thinking style and *never* a feeling style in deciding. You probably use both styles, and such instruments generally designed inform you about which style you prefer to use most often. This is an important part of *orientation;* it guides you in knowing your preferences or patterns of thinking, ways of coming up with ideas, or choices when evaluating or deciding.

Another important aspect of knowing your particular orientation to problem solving is that you have the necessary data to focus on the mutual usefulness of opposite types or styles. Successful problem solving frequently demands the use of a variety of types or styles of thinking, each in the most appropriate place. Personally, you can be aware of your own preferred style and attempt to be flexible in trying to approach a different style when necessary. When you are working in groups, for example, knowing your own style and those of other group members will be helpful in reducing friction and in seeing things from another point of view. All group members may be better able to recognize the similarities and respect the differences among their styles.

There are many other inventories and resources to help you to determine your style of thinking. Many use different conceptions, but can also yield important information about your characteristic strengths, weaknesses, and preferences during problem solving. You need to exercise some caution in using these instruments as they frequently condense much information in an effort to be "quick." This can lead to oversimplification and distortion. Maturity in terms of your orientation involves the capacity to use whatever style is needed when it is needed. In a sense, knowing where you *are* tells you where you *are not,* pointing to the direction in which you have the greatest room to grow.

The following box contains some resources you may wish to consult to get more information about thinking and learning styles.

> Gregorc, A. F. *An Adult's Guide to Style,* Maynard, MA: Gabriel Systems, Inc., 1982.
> Hersey, P. & Natemayer, W. E. *Problem-Solving and Decision-Making Style Inventory,* San Diego, CA: Learning Resources Corp., 1982.
> Hogan, R. C. & Champagne, D. W. *Personal Style Inventory* in Pfeiffer, and Jones *The 1980 Annual Handbook for Group Facilitators* (pp. 89-99) San Diego, CA: University Associates.
> Kolb, D. A.; Rubin, I. M.; and McIntyre, J. M. *Organizational Psychology: An experiential approach,* NJ: Prentice-Hall, 1971.
> Lawrence, G. *People Types and Tiger Stripes: A Practical Guide to Learning Styles,* Gainsville, FL: Center for Applications of Psychological Types, 1979.
> Merrill, D. W. and Reid, R. H. *Personal Styles and Effective Performance,* Radnor, PA: Chitton Book Company, 1981.
> Myers, I. B. *Introduction to Type,* Palo Alto, CA: Consulting Psychologists Press, Inc., 1980.
> Price, G. A.; Dunn, R. & Dunn, K. *Productivity Environmental Preference Survey,* Lawrence, KS: Price Systems, Inc., 1979.
> Silver, H. I. & Hanson, J. R. *Learning Style Inventory,* Morristown, NJ: Hanson, Silver & Associates, 1980.

AWARENESS OF BLOCKS TO CREATIVE THINKING

Another aspect of your orientation to CPS is your awareness of blocks to creative thinking. Many writers have described a variety of categories of blocks to creative thinking. Parnes (1981) indicated that these blocks are so numerous that it would be best to summarize them under two major categories: anxiety about our ideas, and conformity and habit-bound thinking. Shallcross (1981) identified five categories of barriers to creativity including: historical, biological, physiological, sociological and psychological obstacles. Raudsepp (1981) provided a list of "Blocks and Barriers to Creativity" and these fell into the categories of personal blocks, problem-solving blocks, and environmental-organizational blocks. Van-Gundy (1982) provided a chapter entitled "Obstacles to Creative Thinking." The categories he used to describe them were: perceptual, emotional, cultural, environmental, and intellectual/expressive.

It is important to identify blocks to creative thinking because awareness of them is the first step toward overcoming them. You will overcome obstacles more effectively when you are conscious of their presence and impact.

An example of the importance of overcoming obstacles was provided by deBono[1]. The focus of the example is habit bound thinking as a block to creativity. Picture a dog who found a way to get to a bone. Each day, the dog's owner places a bone at a particular spot in the backyard. The dog's first successful attempt to get the bone is to travel, as illustrated, the long way around the fence. Each day, the dog con-

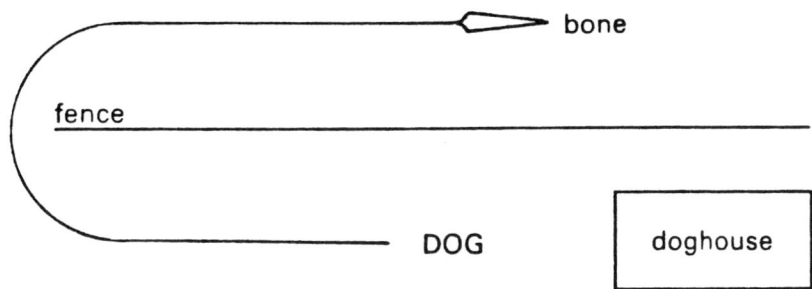

[1] deBono, Edward. Presentation at the 28th Annual Creative Problem-Solving Institute, Buffalo, NY, 1982.

tinues to travel this way to get the bone. This is reinforced every time by getting and enjoying the bone. This pattern of behavior becomes "habit bound." If the dog could ever be made aware of this block, it would then be able to overcome it and discover the shorter route to the desired goal.

But being aware of obstacles is not sufficient to overcome them. A second step is to know and deliberately use a systematic approach to thinking and problem-solving. The appropriate use of these methods may result in effective and novel solutions to problems and challenges. As you become more proficient in using CPS you will also find that you become better able to recognize and overcome obstacles in future situations. Learning and using the process sharpens your overall effectiveness in overcoming blocks to creative thinking.

For example, someone who is drowning will certainly benefit from the application of livesaving techniques. These will be very effective in dealing with the problem at hand (drowning). For that particular crisis, the techniques were of a contingent (unexpected or accidental) nature. A more preventative stance for this problem would be practicing basic swimming skills so the general level of proficiency is improved and drowning is avoided. Learning and practicing basic swimming skills and then anticipating and planning for various obstacles (like cramps, rough water, or panic) provides for better, safer, and more enjoyable swimming. In a sense, learning and practicing basic CPS methods and techniques will help improve your thinking. They can be used to deal with critical matters or to remove unexpected blocks to effective thinking. A more preventative use of CPS is to learn and apply the process as well as being aware of the variety of obstacles you may encounter so they can be anticipated and overcome. In addition, through continuous practice in identifying obstacles to creative thinking and planning to overcome them, a better internalization of CPS strategies will result.

Your knowledge of blocks to creative thinking helps create an internal or personal climate which is supportive of creativity. Some external or environmental factors are also important in establishing and maintaining a climate conducive to creativity. Implementing these conditions helps overcome group or situational blocks. The following twenty suggestions provide a representative list for establishing an atmosphere conducive to creative growth (Isaksen, 1983):

1. Recognize some previously unrecognized and unused potential.
2. Respect an individual's need to work alone; encourage self-initiated projects.
3. Allow and encourage an individual to succeed in an area and in a way possible for him/her.
4. Permit your plan to be different for various individuals; voice the beauty of individual differences.
5. Reduce pressure and provide a nonpunitive environment.
6. Tolerate complexity and disorder, at least for a period.
7. Communicate that you are "for" the individual rather than "against" him/her.
8. Support and reinforce unusual ideas and responses of individuals.
9. Use mistakes as positives to help individuals realize errors and meet acceptable standards in a supportive atmosphere.
10. Adapt to individual interests and ideas whenever possible.
11. Allow time for individuals to think about and develop their creative ideas. Not all creativity occurs immediately and spontaneously.
12. Create a climate of mutual respect and acceptance among individuals so they will share, develop and learn from one another as well as independently.
13. Be aware that creativity is a multi-faceted phenomenon; it enters all curricular areas, not just arts and crafts.
14. Encourage divergent activities by being a resource and a provider rather than a controller.
15. Listen to and laugh with individuals; a warm supportive atmosphere provides freedom and security in exploratory and developmental thinking.
16. Allow individuals to have choices and be part of the decision-making process; let them help control their activities.
17. Let everyone get involved and demonstrate the value of involvement by supporting individual ideas and solutions to problems and projects.
18. Criticism is killing—use it carefully and in small doses.
19. Encourage and use provocative questions; move away from the sole use of convergent, one-answer questions.
20. Don't be afraid to start something different!

The following list of obstacles to creative thinking has been organized into three basic categories. These are: blocks which are primarily personal blocks, problem-solving blocks, or blocks which are situational.

Personal Blocks

The personal obstacles to creativity include those which deal with perceptual limitation and emotional concerns that limit the ability to recognize and deal with new challenges. Certain personality characteristics are included as well.

1. *LACK OF SELF-CONFIDENCE* – The person who lacks self-confidence will fear failure and will avoid risk-taking. Other related fears may include being apprehensive toward criticism and solitude.

2. *A TENDENCY TO CONFORM* – This block promotes a tendency toward comparison and limits access to areas of imagination. This inclination also relates to seeing what you expect to see and results in a failure to utilize all sensory inputs.

3. *A NEED FOR THE FAMILIAR/HABIT BOUND THINKING* – This overriding desire for security and order results in the inability to tolerate ambiguity. There is "no appetite for chaos."

4. *EMOTIONAL "NUMBNESS"* – Situations fail to engage interest. They lack challenge. This promotes reacting to problems rather than being proactive in engaging in preventative problem solving. Being unaware of your feelings means you may lack self-knowledge and be insensitive to a wide spectrum of potential problems.

5. *SATURATION* – This is the tendency to become overly absorbed in a situation (the opposite of incubation). This may result in making false observations and decreased awareness of the "here and now."

6. *EXCESSIVE ENTHUSIASM* – Overmotivation to succeed quickly may result in jumping too soon into problem-solving activity. This extreme zeal may cause a failure to provide the time to use incubation.

7. *LACK OF IMAGINATIVE CONTROL* – This difficulty in having productive access to the use of your imagination limits the kind of thinking you can use. Another result may be an inability to distinguish reality from fantasy.

Problem Solving Blocks

Obstacles to creative problem solving relate to an individual's processing abilities and skills which hinder effective outcomes. These problem-solving blocks deal more with the cognitive or thinking activities which hamper the attainment of new and useful solutions to problems.

1. *SOLUTION FIXEDNESS* – This block relates to the one-sided emphasis on finding the answer than to solving the problem (quick-fix). This type of fixedness causes you to grab and use the first idea rather than developing a pool of alternatives to choose from. A related symptom is the intolerance of complexity.

2. *PREMATURE JUDGMENTS* – This is a common barrier to creative thinking. It is associated with an inability to suspend judgment and an inordinate emphasis on judgment over generation of ideas. This is frequently illustrated by the individual who must have only ideas that are concrete, practical and in finished form.

3. *HABIT TRANSFER* – When a mental set exists which offers previously successful strategies as useful for new and different situations, other even more effective strategies are frequently overlooked. The killer phrase "We've *always* done it this way!" sums up the block pretty well.

4. *USE OF POOR APPROACHES* – Working with inadequate, incorrect, or insufficient information may mislead you. Using an incorrect problem definition will take you off course. Seeing only a narrow aspect of the problem situation rather than a variety of viewpoints limits effectiveness and may result in difficulty in isolating the "real" problem. Sometimes taking an overly adaptive stance lulls you into remaining within "obvious" boundaries of a problem. There are many potentially unproductive approaches to effective problem solving.

5. *LACK OF DISCIPLINED EFFORT* – The myth that creative problem-solving is easy may be frequently put aside when people work on meaningful challenges. Certain aspects of the process may be fun, but as Sid Parnes has said "it's not *for* fun."

6. *POOR LANGUAGE SKILL* – Use of an inadequate or inappropriate language to solve a problem would be inefficient and probably not produce a suitable outcome. For example, using a mathematical/analytical language for a problem requiring a visual language may result in a non-productive use of your energy.

7. *RIGIDITY* – The inability of a person or group to switch from one problem-solving approach to another blocks the flexible use of a variety of strategies and techniques which may be necessary.

Situational Blocks

Situational blocks to creative thinking include the elements of the immediate environment as well as the cultural or sociological aspects. These blocks frequently combine with the other types listed above. For example, the internal and personal obstacle such as the fear of being seen as strange will interact with the use by others of "killer phrases" to result in decreasing the likelihood of suggesting a new and better idea.

1. *SCIENTIFIC REASONING PROVIDES A PANACEA* – This attitude promotes the view that reason, logic, numbers utility, practicality and tradition are good; feeling, intuition, qualitative judgments, pleasure and change are bad. Playfulness is seen as appropriate for children only, fantasy and reflection are a waste of time. The resulting opinion is that problem solving is a serious business and that humor is out of place. This belief violates the "delicate balance" needed for creativity.

2. *RESISTANCE TO NEW IDEAS* – This resistance is usually observed in the form of criticism of new ideas. Newness and novelty are perceived as threats to security and status. Maintaining the status quo is of primary concern and there is a lack of interest in identifying problems. This block provides a large reservoir for killer phrases like "That will never work," "That idea will cost too much!" or "We've never done it that way before!"

3. *ISOLATION* – Departmentalization of thinking, excessive and limited ownership over ideas, excessive organizational friction and a climate where others don't get involved in your problem solving greatly limits the amount of intellectual resources focused on solving problems.

4. *NEGATIVE ATTITUDE TOWARD CREATIVE THINKING* – There may be plenty of time for work but no time for creative thinking. Other titles for this condition are "smugnosis" or "psychosclerosis."

5. *AUTOCRATIC DECISION MAKING* – Repeated use of top-down decision-making may result in quieting a questioning attitude. This may cut off many opportunities for productive thinking.

6. *EXPERTS* – The dependency or over-reliance on others to continuously solve your problems places a great deal of emphasis outside your ability area. Although experts can provide some excellent guidance and information, you should be careful not to rely on them

for all problem-solving efforts. Even experts in your own group may have an inappropriate amount of influence in decision making.

7. *AN OVER-EMPHASIS ON COMPETITION OR COOPERATION* – Both competition and cooperation are important elements of personal and group functioning. Some use of each appears to be necessary for many healthy accomplishments. Focusing too much on either one may cause you to lose sight of the problem. In essence, an excessive amount of consideration given to the relationship aspect of group relations over the task aspect may be unproductive (certainly the reverse is true also . . . back to that "dynamic balance" again!).

Because so much has been written about blocks to creative thinking and we have only provided a brief introduction to the topic. You may find it helpful to study some of these references.

> Biondi, A. M. "About the Small Cage Habit . . . ", *Journal of Creative Behavior*, Volume 14, Number 2, 1980, pp. 75-76.
> Maslow, A. H. "Emotional Blocks to Creativity" in Parnes and Harding *A Sourcebook for Creative Thinking*, NY: Scribners, 1962, pp. 93-103.
> Parnes, S. J. *The Magic of Your Mind*, Buffalo, NY: CEF & Bearly Ltd. 1981.
> Raudsepp, E. *How Creative Are You*, (Part II: Blocks and Barriers to Creativity, pp. 45-102) NYC: Perigree Books, 1981.
> Shallcross, D. J. *Teaching Creative Behavior*, Englewood Cliffs, NJ: Prentice-Hall Inc., 1981.
> Tumin, M. "Obstacles to Creativity" in Parnes and Harding *A Sourcebook for Creative Thinking*, NY: Scribners, 1962, pp. 105-113.
> Turecamo, D. "How to Murder an Idea", *Kiwanis Magazine*, March 1983, pp. 16-19.
> VanGundy, A. B. *Training Your Creative Mind* (Chapter 2: Obstacles to Creative Thinking, Englewood Cliffs, NJ: Prentice Hall, 1982, pp. 12-41.

DIVERGENCE IN MESS-FINDING

Outcomes and Obstacles

To generate a variety of Mess statements, you may focus on outcomes and obstacles. *Outcomes* focus on goals or end results you hope for; these are objectives or things you need or want. *Obstacles* are things, people, or events which stand in the way of attaining some desired outcome. They are the trouble spots that hamper our efforts.

When diverging during Mess-Finding, you may find it helpful to make a list of outcomes you want to attain or obstacles you want to remove. Whether you focus your energy on *producing outcomes* or *removing obstacles*, it will be productive to have a variety of options from which to choose.

These elements of Mess-Finding deal with how you view the situation. Is the situation primarily a "challenge" or "opportunity," or is it a "threat, crisis or emergency?" This knowledge will set the tone and perhaps determine the pace of your efforts with the Mess. In addition, this knowledge may help you to decide what kind(s) of change(s) you're seeking.

If you focus on producing outcomes you may be viewing the situation as a challenge. To generate a variety of messes, answer the question: *"Wouldn't it be nice if . . .?"* (WIBNI). If most of your energy is devoted to identifying or removing obstacles, your view could be that the mess is a threat or annoyance. To develop a diversity of statements from this point of view, answer the question: *"Wouldn't it be awful if . . .?"* (WIBAI). You will find that we often use different words to describe different orientations. For example, see the table below and the words that may be associated with both positions.

	+ (WIBNI)	Neutral	(WIBAI)[2] –
WHAT	Encouragement Opportunity Challenge	Circumstance Event Puzzle	Worry Problem Fear

[2] We express our appreciation to Dr. James J. Gallagher, University of North Carolina, for suggesting the phrase, "WIBAI . . . ?"

	+ (WIBNI)	Neutral	(WIBAI)² −
	Desire Wish/hope/dream "Good chance"	Paradox Perplexing Need/Want	Threat Concern Frustration
WHO	Friends Supporters Assister Pal/Buddies Life Lines	Relatives Yourself Employer Advisors Peers Customer Client Boss	Enemies Opponents Resister Pests Nuisances
WHERE	Special Place Hideaway Retreat Vacation	Home School Job Community (etc.)	Accident Mess Trouble Spot
WHEN	Target Schedule Smooth Relaxed Systematic Comfortable	Job Time Study Time Leisure Time Meal Time	Frantic Rushed Late Overdue Hassled Harried
WHY	Extend Increase/Improve Want to/Choose Expand/Enhance Growth Excitement Invent Enjoy	Maintain Substitute Combine Eliminate Replace	Overlooked Fix/Repair Boredom Have to/Must Survive Salvage Get it over with Put up with
HOW	Eagerly Happy Anticipation Tease/Tantalize Stimulating Exciting	My Way	Reluctantly Sadly Dread Nagging/Bugging Aggravating Irritating

Guidelines for effective "Mess" statements

To help you generate a goal that can be productively approached through the use of CPS, the following guidelines should be helpful:

1. *BROAD* – keep your "Mess" statement general so that you don't prematurely attempt to "define the problem" or "search for *the* solution."

2. *BRIEF* – limit the number of words used so the statement can be dealt with in "headline" form.

3. *BENEFICIAL* – although often you want to frame the statement to remove an obstacle, try to state it in a positive or affirmative manner.

Some examples of mess generating prefaces include:

> If I had my way . . .
> If I could do anything, I would . . .
> If I were king (queen) . . .
> If I had a magic wand I would . . .
> I wish . . .
> I hope . . .
> I'd really like . . .
> It would sure be helpful if . . .
> Why don't we . . .
> Let's consider . . .
> I wonder if we could . . .
> It would make my day if . . .

Diverging Activities

There are many ways to generate a variety of mess statements and many variables that influence how many and what kind of statements we develop. The following divergent activities are designed to help you produce and discover profitable directions for your problem-solving efforts. Before evaluating where you want to go, it is important to generate your options.

The first activity is the Mess-Finding Matrix. This matrix combines the aspects of your personal orientation to problem solving and your situational outlook. Use the questions within the quadrants to generate several possible situations for your attention.

The second activity is the Wallet Checklist. This activity encourages you to generate a variety of possible areas for personal action by re-discovering some artifacts you carry around most of the time.

Creative Problem Solving: The Basic Course

DMF-1: MESS-FINDING MATRIX

I. Fill in the four quadrants of this matrix to help you generate a number of different challenges and situations from which to choose.

PERSONAL ORIENTATION

	Strengths	Weaknesses
Outcomes	What opportunities do I want to consider? What do I hope to accomplish? What personal strengths do I want to improve on to use to deal with this opportunity?	What opportunities are difficult to work on because of some personal limitation? What weaknesses do I want to focus on improving (or choose to deal with) to accomplish what I want to?
Obstacles	What are some obstacles I feel I can deal with? What is preventing me from doing what I want? What personal strengths do I want to use (or improve upon) to deal with the(se) concern(s)?	What limitations, or lack of resources (personal or situational) do I want to improve or work on?

(Left axis label: **SITUATIONAL OUTLOOK**)

II. Examine what you have written and choose an area of importance for you. Form a "fuzzy" general statement of this Mess using about 20 words.

DMF-2: WALLET CHECKLIST

Sometimes you are fortunate enough to have a clear idea of what Mess you want to work on. More often one carries around several concerns which seem to be of competing importance. Imagine an airport baggage claim area: all the bags are moving around on a conveyor and you are having difficulty picking out your own. When you have several thoughts or concerns on your mind, deciding on what to do can be as confusing as picking out the right bag. This state of confusion can be as frustrating as some of the "Messes" themselves. So what can you do to get started? This is an exercise to help generate and list a variety of messes. Your wallet can be a handy source of some areas of concern, where you can begin to identify "Messes." The items inside are like claim checks or tags to help identify your baggage.

Wallets are often a reflection of ourselves, containing those things that are important or greatly valued to us. For example, a person rummaging through his/her wallet may discover quite a variety of things:

- photographs of family or friends
- phone numbers and addresses
- identification such as employment cards, driver's license, club membership, health care programs, bank accounts, social security, voter registration
- coupons, bills or receipts
- mementos

From the contents, one item might attract particular attention. Perhaps it is something you feel needs more attention. Suppose, for example, you selected a health care identification card.

While holding the card and looking at it, several thoughts may come to mind.

Thoughts
"Have a physical."
"Lose weight."
"Remember to take my vitamins."
"Eat more nutritious meals."
"Get new glasses and an eye examination."
"Find time and motivation to exercise."

Using these thoughts as a source, you can now form a list of Messes to consider. Use the guidelines for effective Mess statements (pages 32 and 33 in this chapter) to phrase your Mess statements so they will emphasize your goals or desires. From your health care card thoughts, for example, you might make these Mess statements.

Thought	**Mess**
Have a physical	Get in shape
Like to lose weight	Improve my appearance
Take my vitamins	Be more conscious of good health
Eat more nutritious meals	Improve eating habits
Find time and motivation	Health maintenance plan

Directions: Take your own wallet, pick an item, and follow the procedure outlined above.

Thoughts	Mess

CONVERGENCE IN MESS-FINDING

The convergent phase provides some rating of importance for the variety of messes generated during the divergent phase and focuses our problem-solving efforts.

The convergent phase of Mess-Finding involves determining your ownership and outlook related to a challenge. Converging during Mess-Finding ensures that you select a challenge you own and that you work on solving something of personal importance. This phase of Mess-Finding provides an opportunity to evaluate and analyze various situations to select or build one with some personal priority. You have the chance to separate some of the key elements and decide which are most important to consider.

Ownership

If you're going to put your energy into problem solving, it is important to work on a situation for which you really want a solution! That's called "ownership." There are varying degrees of ownership, which can change from challenge to challenge. To demonstrate these levels of ownership, let's use an analogy from business to describe varying levels of ownership so they parallel different types of enterprise. The "sole proprietorship" is the kind of Mess for which a single client has *all* the ownership. He or she assumes all the responsibility for making decisions during the process and for carrying out the resulting plans. The "partnership" is a situation with two or more owners. Decision-making and implementation responsibility are shared by the partners. The third and most diverse type of ownership can be compared with the "corporation." The "corporate Mess" allows many to share ownership. Some may have more "stock" in the Mess than others, and some may be more involved than others in carrying out the decisions. These guidelines can help you check ownership, and assure productive use of your problem-solving energies:

1. *INFLUENCE.* Is this a situation for which you have some explicit authority and decision-making responsibility? (Do you have the "clout" for this Mess?)
2. *INTEREST.* Are you *willing* to submit the challenge to systematic problem-solving efforts? (Motivation; do you care enough to follow through?)
3. *IMAGINATION.* Are you looking for something really new and meaningful? (Is there room for openness and novelty?)

Usually you will answer "yes" to each of these three questions. If you are contemplating using CPS for a Mess lacking any of these elements of ownership, you may end up with a solution without anyone to use it or a plan which doesn't strike you as one worth the effort involved. Therefore, it is important to be certain that someone has ownership of the results of the Mess. Someone (preferably you!) should *want* to attain an innovative plan and a way to carry it out. This helps to ensure that your time, effort, and energy invested in the process will be worthwhile.

If your ownership is limited, it would be advisable to modify the situation to maximize your ownership or to avoid the problem altogether. For example, the Mess of the threat of nuclear war may provide adequate imagination and interest, but you have inadequate influence. You might simply choose to withdraw from a systematic approach or you may break down the Mess into parts for which you may have more influence. In this case you may choose to communicate your concerns about nuclear war or taking some political action to deal with the problem. By identifying your level of ownership, you can "massage" (modify to suit your needs) the Mess to a point where you ultimately identify an adequate level of ownership to justify continuing work with the process.

Outlook

After you have determined your ownership of a Mess, the next step is to assess your particular viewpoint about the challenge. This is called your *outlook*. Part of your outlook refers to your awareness of knowledge and information about the general mess area.

Examining your outlook during Mess-Finding provides information about the time frame for your problem-solving efforts and assists in determining where to start. Knowing your outlook toward a challenge will help you sort out your "Mess" by separating and prioritizing elements of the situation at hand.

The view you hold about a situation helps to prioritize the elements of the Mess. To prioritize concerns or objectives you can examine the critical nature, immediacy and stability of the situation. These considerations also provide input into deciding where to begin your systematic efforts. This activity will help you in converging on the most appropriate situational definition for your problem-solving energies.

1. *FAMILIARITY* – To assure productive results for your involvement in CPS, you need to assess your general level of knowledge regarding the problem area. If the Mess is one about which you really don't have much relevant information, then your early working time should be spent gathering basic data or background information. In addition, it is helpful to do some investigating to find out what resources are available (time, money, etc.) to meet the challenge. For example, being knowledgeable about the challenge from the beginning helps you to answer important questions during the Data-Finding stage. It also assists you in formulating important questions about the Mess itself, and in making decisions about how to plan your problem-solving efforts.

2. *CRITICAL NATURE* – To assess the critical nature of the Mess, examine the situation's importance. If you consider the Mess a relatively trivial item, it would be assigned a low priority. However, if you regard the situation as very important with serious consequences, you would assign it a high priority.

3. *IMMEDIACY* – To determine the level of immediacy, examine how soon initial action must be taken. Some messes may require that initial action take place in the long range (a month or so). Some messes may dictate a shorter range (about two weeks) for initial action to be taken. Still others may require immediate action.

4. *DIRECTION* – Prioritizing elements of the mess also takes into account the situation's stability. This consideration examines what will happen to this situation over time. Some situations may stay the same or even improve if left alone for awhile. A higher priority may be assigned for a situation that will worsen over time. In terms of outlook, situations of great importance which need to be dealt with immediately and could get worse over time require your highest priority.

Converging Activities

Converging during Mess-Finding involves evaluating or rating the appropriateness and significance of the variety of mess statements you generated during the divergent phase. To assist in these efforts, use the Mess-Finding Checklist on the following pages.

Creative Problem Solving: The Basic Course

CMF-1: MESS-FINDING CHECKLIST

```
┌─────────────────────────────────────────────────────────────────────────┐
│  BRIEF STATEMENT OF MESS YOU HAVE CHOSEN:                               │
│                                                                         │
│                                                                         │
│                                                                         │
│                                                                         │
│                                                                         │
└─────────────────────────────────────────────────────────────────────────┘
```

You will be able to use CPS successfully if you find you have influence, interest and imagination for this Mess.

USE YOUR BRIEF STATEMENT TO . . .

Check for Ownership:

1. *INFLUENCE:* Is this a situation for which you have some responsibility and decision-making authority? _____

    *If *yes,* continue to respond to remaining questions.

    *If *no* or *don't know,* can you restate (massage) your Mess so that you can clearly claim some personal "clout" for some aspect of the situation? If not, you may benefit from working on something else.

2. *INTEREST:* Are you willing and interested enough to submit this challenge to systematic efforts to achieve a solution? _____

    *If *yes,* continue to respond to the remaining questions.

    *If *no* or *don't know,* then you may have selected a mess that doesn't really intrigue you. Can you locate some aspect of the Mess that you would be motivated to work on? If not, you may benefit from working on something else.

3. *IMAGINATION:* Are you looking for something new, a different view, or a novel approach? _____

    *If *yes,* continue to the remaining sections of this checklist.

    *If *no* or *don't know,* then you may not need to use all the CPS stages for this mess. After you have developed your skill in using CPS, you may find that for *some* messes only certain stages are necessary. Can you restate your mess so you are searching for new or different perspectives? If not, then you may actually be better off choosing a different challenge on which to work at this time.

Check Your Outlook:

1. *FAMILIARITY:* Do I have a general awareness of the area? Do I have enough knowledge of the subject so I can identify key facts or raise important questions to find relevant data?

    _____ Yes, I think I know enough to continue.

    _____ This is something I need to pay special attention to (research, find a partner, read, ask questions, hire a consultant, etc.)

2. *CRITICAL NATURE:* How important do you consider this mess? (Place an "x" on the appropriate place on the line.)

   (Low Priority)_____(High Priority)

   Trivial   Of some interest   Very important;
                                  and concern   Serious consequences

3. *IMMEDIACY:* How soon would you say you must take initial action:

   (Low Priority)_____(High Priority)

   May start something   Should start   Must start
   in the distant future   shortly   immediately

4. *DIRECTION:* How will this situation change over time?

   (Low Priority)_____(High Priority)

   Improve if left alone?   Stay the same   Get worse if left alone?
                                  if left alone?

If you have ownership for the situation and have examined your outlook, you are ready to proceed with the next stages of the process.

REFERENCES CITED

Ainsworth-Land, G. & V. *The opportunity discovery process* Buffalo, NY: D.O.K. Publishers, 1982.

Campbell, D. *If you don't know where you're going you'll probably end up somewhere else* Allen, TX: Argus Communications, 1984.

Carey, R. L. "Fuzzy Analysis in Creative Problem Solving" *G/C/T,* Mar./Apr., 1984, pp. 25-27.

Isaksen, S. G. "Toward a Model for the facilitation of creative problem solving", *Journal of Creative Behavior,* Volume 17, Number 1, 1983, pp. 18-31.

Kaufman, R. *Identifying and solving problems: a system approach* San Diego, CA: University Associates, 1982.

Koberg, D. & Bagnall, J. *The All New Universal Traveler: a soft systems guide to creativity, problem solving and the process of reaching goals,* Los Altos, CA: William Kaufmann, 1981.

MacKinnon, D. W. *In search of human effectiveness: Identifying and developing creativity.* Buffalo, NY: Bearly Ltd., 1978.

Mager, R. F. *Goal Analysis* Belmont, CA: Pitman Learning, Inc., 1974.

Mager, R. F. & Pipe, P. *Analyzing Performance Problems* Belmont, CA: Pitman Learning, Inc., 1970.

CHAPTER 4

Data-Finding

> **Data-Finding Stage**
>
> The situation is examined from different viewpoints to gather information, impressions, perceptions, feelings. The most important data are identified and analyzed.

After studying this chapter, you will be able to:

1. Explain Data-Finding and its importance in the CPS process.
2. Define five different kinds of data, give examples of them and differentiate among them.
3. Distinguish between data that represent **known** or **given** information about a Mess and data that represent **needed** or **wanted** information.
4. Use observation and all the senses more effectively in Data-Finding.
5. Describe and use a variety of methods and techniques for generating, analyzing and testing data for any Mess.
6. Describe and use specific Data-Finding questions and checklists to examine and analyze data for any Mess.
7. Describe and use several methods and Data-Finding Matrixes for evaluating, prioritizing and selecting data for any Mess.
8. Apply Data-Finding methods and techniques when working on a Mess of your own.

Data-Finding

Once you've found a Mess that is really interesting, you're probably eager to get right into the process of creative problem solving. You want to get down to the business of solving the problem—the sooner, the better. But, *please,* wait a minute so you won't get into trouble. Many people go astray here. Pansy Torrance was the first colleague we heard saying "the only exercise some minds get is jumping to conclusions." Jumping from the Mess to a solution can mean trouble. You may find you have a nice answer to a question no one asked. Some people say, "Oh, I *already know* what the problem is . . . . ," but often, after spending several frustrating hours, they discover that the *real* problem was actually quite different. (There are also *some* folks, unfortunately, who just say, "My mind is made up; don't confuse me with facts!" They usually get what they deserve.)

A very simple example of the need for data-finding has been used (with many variations) as the basis for comedy sketches: a person is preparing to enjoy watching television. When he or she turns on the set, however, nothing happens. After fiddling with the switch, banging the side of the set, and various other frustrated actions, the person calls the TV Service Company. Isn't it embarrassing and frustrating (not to mention expensive) when the repair person points out to you that the set wasn't plugged into the wall?

Some data-finding will always help you to improve your effectiveness in understanding the problems that really need to be solved.

To help you become a more effective problem solver and to avoid some of these "traps," this chapter will present some specific methods and techniques for taking a closer look at your mess. We call this stage, "Data-Finding."

WHAT IS DATA-FINDING?

The purpose of Data-Finding is to help you explore all the information, impressions, observations, feelings, and questions that you have about a Mess on which you've decided to work.

Every Mess, and the situation surrounding it, contains a vast array of information and data. In most situations, there will be considerably more data available than you will usually be able to recognize or use. Some of these data may not really be very important, of course. For example, if you're thinking about how to organize the books in your personal library, the observation that there's a grey, cloudy sky outside may be irrelevant. If you were considering whether or not to go out to play tennis, however, the weather and sky conditions would be much more important.

Divergent thinking during Data-Finding is a necessary first step. It helps you to avoid overlooking important information. But it also helps you to recognize or discover some important information that you hadn't thought about, or that might too easily have been dismissed as irrelevant or unimportant. Finding something unexpected but important often results from doing a thorough job during the "divergent" phase of Data-Finding.

Several kinds of "input" or "raw material" are important to consider during Data-Finding. We use the word "data" because it is a general term that encompasses many different sources of information or kinds of input. Five different kinds of data might be included in your Data-Finding efforts. These are:

1. *INFORMATION.* Recognition, recall, and use of knowledge derived from study, experience, or instruction; knowledge of specific events, people, places, or situations; news; what is known and can be perceived, calculated, verified, discovered, or inferred.

2. *IMPRESSIONS.* Images or effects retained as a consequence of experience and/or beliefs; hunches, notions, or intuitive cognitions.

3. *OBSERVATIONS.* The act of noting, taking into account, and recording information through the senses.

Creative Problem Solving: The Basic Course

4. *FEELINGS.* Sensitivity or awareness of information or data through emotions, sentiments, or affective responses.

5. *QUESTIONS.* Expressions of inquiry, based on uncertainty, lack of information, or curiosity, that call for data.

Figure IV-1. Sources of Data

INFORMATION
knowledge
facts
intelligence
memory
comprehend
recollection

IMPRESSIONS
intuitive guess
hunch
image
reasonable expectation
belief
vague notion

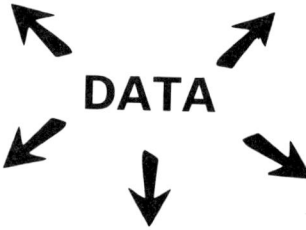

FEELINGS
emotions
sentiment
awareness
affective
desire
sensitivity
sympathy/empathy

OBSERVATIONS
notice
watch
perception
comment
take into account

QUESTIONS
inquiry
doubt
perplexity
difficulty
uncertainty
curiosities

The "converging" steps in the Mess-Finding Chapter provided you with some of the data you'll be exploring in greater detail in this stage. As you examined your Outlook on the Mess, for example, you established certain priorities that will guide you in this stage. It might be helpful to compare the Mess to a diamond in the rough. It has great merit and value locked within, but until we've worked with it, that value cannot be realized. The skillful diamond cutter must examine the stone patiently, measuring, weighing, looking at it from every angle, to prepare it for the precise break that will unlock the gem's brilliance and beauty. You will need to examine your Mess from many different perspectives, too, looking for the data that will unlock the most productive way of stating problems or sub-problems in later stages.

You will need to search for important data about your Mess from many different angles and viewpoints, trying to make some observations and "connections" to help you better to understand what the Mess really involves. You will need to develop your skill at noticing things that are usually overlooked, and at looking at familiar ideas and things in strange and unusual ways. You will need to "sharpen your senses" to heighten your awareness and to become sensitive to small details that may be important. You should try to sort out what you *know* about the Mess, what you *need to know,* and what you'd *like to know.*

KNOW = Information already available to you

NEED TO KNOW = The "musts" that are needed to help you understand the mess.

LIKE TO KNOW = The "wants" that would be nice to help you fill out your picture of the mess.

WHY IS DATA-FINDING IMPORTANT?

Data-Finding is a very important stage of CPS for several reasons. It helps us to:

1. break away from stereotyped or habit-bound thinking.
2. uncover key pieces of information about the Mess that might have been obscured, overlooked, or so obvious that they went unnoticed.
3. "take stock" of the situation by sorting out just what we really do and don't know about the Mess, thereby helping us avoid premature closure.
4. determine our PRIMARY PRIORITIES–the parts of the Mess that stand out and really demand some attention and action.
5. look at the Mess as broadly as possible, stretching ourselves to consider data in many ways.
6. "unlock" hidden patterns or interrelationships among data in the general situation–patterns that we may not have considered previously.
7. create a reasonable basis for prioritizing and making decisions about how to structure and analyze the Mess.
8. establish and maintain a focus on the *process* that we are employing.
9. examine and test the relative strength or value of various components of a Mess so we can clarify our viewpoints and establish priorities for dealing effectively with the components.
10. remove "blinders" caused by assumptions.

Data-Finding helps "soften up" the Mess–to prepare it for productive problem solving. For example, the following problem was recently brought up by a participant in a workshop with the authors:

I decided to come to this workshop (in California) even though my home is in New England. I want to be able to take the messages from my office telephone answering machine, but I accidentally destroyed the "code" in my remote control unit that triggers the machine by phone, and without the machine, I can't reset the code.

She saw the Mess as being unable to get the messages from the machine. We began to consider some Data-Finding questions:

What do you need to reset the code?	My answering machine, but it's home.
What kind of machine is it?	She named it–a well-known, national brand.
Can any machine of that brand be used to reset the code?	I suppose so.
Is there a store near our Hotel that sells this machine?	I don't know.
How can we find out?	Check the phone book or ask at the Hotel desk.

There was a store that carried the same machine–in a small plaza less than 100 yards from the room in which we were meeting, as it turned out–and by noon the next day, a machine had been borrowed, the code reestablished in the remote control unit, and the messages successfully obtained from the machine at home.

GETTING STARTED IN DATA-FINDING

Let's try several exercises to help you learn some useful methods and techniques for Data-Finding. First, you'll have an opportunity to try some activities to help in your efforts to *diverge* in Data-Finding, and to *stretch* your approach to a Mess in order to collect as much data as possible. Then, you'll learn and practice specific methods to help you *converge* or identify the most significant data to carry forward into the next stage of CPS (Problem-Finding).

Diverging Activities:

The following pages contain some diverging Data-Finding Activities.

DDF-1: LOOK AND SEE

Most of us look at more than we see! We often allow habits or perceptual expectations to "trap" us into being unable to observe closely. Effective Data-Finding demands that you become a good observer—to look closely at the situation, to notice new elements and relationships, and to "see" aspects of the situation.

Study the drawing:

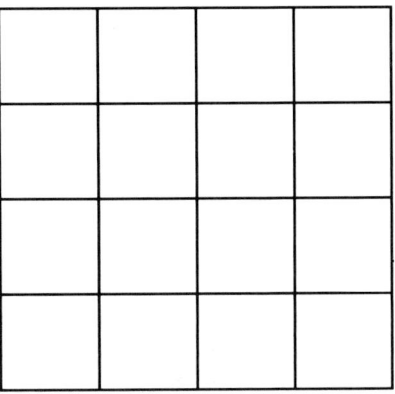

How many squares do you see? _____
Did you say 16–or even 17? Keep looking!
S-T-R-E-T-C-H your powers of observation. Look at the drawing from another angle, or slide a piece of paper over it from left to right, or from top to bottom. Can you find some additional squares that you overlooked initially?
How many squares do you see now? _____
If you said 22, 23, or even 29–keep looking!
We aren't going to give you any "right answer" for the Exercise. Perhaps an anecdote will help you understand why.
A little boy once said to one of us, "I see an *infinite* number of squares." When pressed to explain his response, he said, "Think of it as a long tube–like a hose, but square instead of round, and infinitely long. I'm just looking at one end–the top row of squares, but they keep going and going." *Now* how many squares can you find? Explain your connection:

_____

Explain your connection:

_____

_____

_____

_____

_____

_____

DDF-2: MEET THE PEANUT

Millions of people enjoy roasted peanuts. It's fun to crack open the shells and eat the tasty nuts. But have you ever looked very closely at the peanut?

Examine the picture below, or better yet, get a handful of roasted peanuts in the shell. Study the peanut carefully. Try to make as many observations about it as you can.

Figure IV-2.

List some of your observations:

_____
_____
_____
_____
_____
_____
_____
_____
_____
_____
_____

Have you really *stretched?* What have you really observed about the peanut? Several high school students we've known have made 50 or more observations—on just the *outside* of the peanut!

What kinds of information can you get from . . . .

    . . . . touching the peanut?

                                          texture
                                          shape
                                          sharp/dull
                                          temperature, etc.

        . . . . smelling? . . . . listening? . . . . watching?

Look back at other kinds of information—from the words in Figure IV-1 (page 44 in this chapter). What other *means* can you use to gather data about the peanut? What other *kinds* of information will those means help you to obtain? List even MORE observations:

_____ _____
_____ _____
_____ _____
_____ _____

Now, really STRETCH. Surprise yourself with how much you can observe about the peanut that you've never noticed in "all your previous meetings." Perhaps these words will help trigger new and unusual observations for you:

sight	sound	taste	touch	smell
color	rattle	saline	hard	aroma
distance	tone	sweet	soft	burnt
density	tempo	bland	rough	fragrance
structure	noise	tangy	smooth	clean
speed	range	dry	size	earthy
contrast	depth	fruity	sticky	ferment
focus	vibrate	raw	powdery	smoky
line	clunk	sour	wet	new
shade	discord	spicy	fuzzy	musty

Other objects which could be used for this exercise include: oranges, radios, nail clippers, watches, plastic bandages, etc. Try another object to compare your ability to observe effectively.

DDF-3: OBSERVATION GUIDE

Let's take a common object and try to look at it in many ways. Try to experience it in many different ways–try to change your perspective and describe it from viewpoints that you have never thought about before!

WHAT DO YOU . . . . .

SEE	TASTE	SMELL

HEAR	TOUCH/FEEL	DESCRIBE OTHER WAYS

DDF-4: THE ALL-PURPOSE HELPER

Wouldn't it be great if everyone had an "all purpose helper" like the one shown in the picture below?

Figure IV-3.

What kinds of Data are available about the All-Purpose Helper? What is it like, and what can it do?

WHAT ARE SOME . . . . .

. . . . "OBVIOUS FACTS?" Describe what you see	. . . . "REASONABLE INFERENCES?" Work from your observations
_____	_____
_____	_____
_____	_____
_____	_____
_____	_____
_____	_____
_____	_____
_____	_____

Let's look for even MORE data about the All-Purpose Helper.

WHAT "WILD GUESSES" CAN YOU MAKE?	WHAT PUZZLES OR PERPLEXES YOU?
Offer some speculations, feelings, hunches about it	What questions might you want to ask?

_____   _____

_____   _____

_____   _____

_____   _____

_____   _____

_____   _____

_____   _____

Do you think everyone in a group would see the same things or make the same observations that you did? (Discuss this with other members of a group, or share the exercise with some friends and get their reactions.)

_____

_____

_____

What do you expect might be sources of agreement among most people who look at the picture?

_____

_____

_____

_____

About what might there be the greatest degree of difference among several viewers?

_____

_____

_____

_____

_____

DDF-5: STRANGER THAN FICTION

Everytime you read a newspaper or a news magazine or watch the news on television, you're a "data collector." If you're really paying attention, there's a great deal of information for you in any story.

Directions:
Read the article on the right side of this page.

Underline or highlight the data that you find.

Look for even more data; how much data can you extract from this brief article?

Be sure to consider some new, varied, or unusual perspectives—remember that there are many kinds of "data!"

Anyone want 15 tons of old money?
The Associated Press

ATLANTA—The Atlanta Federal Reserve Bank throws away 15 tons of money each month—shredded, of course—and officials are looking for someone to recycle the old bills.

Bank spokesman Duane W. Kline says the bank has been hauling the destroyed money to landfills, but it would like to find a more useful, less costly way to get rid of the paper.

"There's a general appreciation these days of recycling whenever possible," Kline said in a recent interview. Some companies use the money in novelty items, such as ball point pens and paper weights, but that market is limited, he said.

Attempts to use the shreds in making particle board and roofing material haven't been very efficient, Kline said. And the Treasury Department won't allow the cash to be used to make more paper, since the resulting product would be ideal for would-be counterfeiters.

Kline suggested the money might be used for insulation, but he knows of no one who has tried that.

One difficulty in disposing of the money the Treasury Department requires the buyer to take the whole 15-ton load each month.

Reprinted by permission of AP.

Use this page to note data that you found in the article; add extra pages as you need them.

_____

_____

_____

_____

Did you really stretch?
Compare your Data-Finding efforts with ours by reading the next page. Did we locate some data that you missed? Did you uncover some data that escaped our attention?

Some Data We Found From the Story....

1. Atlanta
2. Federal Reserve Bank
3. Discards
4. 15 tons
5. Money (U.S. Currency)
6. Each month
7. Shreds it first
8. Officials involved
9. Looking for someone
10. Recycle shredded bills
11. Bills old when shredded
12. Duane W. Kline speaks for the Bank
13. Money has been hauled
14. To landfills
15. Bank wants more useful idea
16. Bank must get rid of shredded paper.
17. Bank wants reduced cost
18. Kline was interviewed
19. Recently
20. Relates problem to general interest in recycling
21. They know *some* uses
22. Novelty ball point pens
23. Novelty paperweights
24. Novelty market is limited
25. Practical uses tried
26. Particle board
27. Roofing materials
28. Kline says these weren't efficient
29. Treasury Dept. involved
30. Treasury Dept. has rules
31. Can't use it for making paper
32. Such paper too good
33. Might encourage counterfeiters
34. Kline's idea: use in insulation
35. No one he knows has tried it
36. One "string" attached
37. Another Treasury Dept. rule
38. Buyer (won't give it away?)
39. Required to take all 15 tons
40. Each month!
41. Article has seven word title
42. Six paragraphs
43. Eight sentences
44. Story by Associated Press
45. Story from Atlanta office
46. 185 words
47. Article about 2½" x 5" in size
48. No byline or author credit
49. Sentences range from 16 words to 34 words
50. Average sentence length = 23 words
51. Three letters of alphabet not used (J, X, Z)
52. Three contractions
53. Two hyphenated words
54. Nine commas
55. One direct quotation
56. One colon and no semi-colons
57. Three dashes

DDF-6: FIVE W's AND AN H

Your Data-Finding efforts will become easier and more successful if you learn to use several "key words" to help yourself. These key words (–five W's and an H–) are: Who, What, Where, When, Why, and How. These questions help in different ways during Data-Finding.

WHO helps you to identify everyone (individuals or groups) who might be involved in the Mess.

WHAT helps identify all the things, materials, resources, objects, or items involved in the Mess.

WHERE considers the areas, places, locations, positions, or focal points in the Mess.

WHEN probes the times, intervals, schedules, dates, beginnings, endings, or deadlines in the Mess.

WHY inquires about the reasons, goals, aims, or intentions in the Mess.

HOW helps you to recognize previous actions that have been attempted, things that are now occurring, and steps that might be taken.

Use these words to formulate questions to help you explore every possible angle or aspect of your Mess. In the divergent phase of Data-Finding, you want to avoid overlooking *any* information that might be helpful in understanding the situation and eventually lead to constructive, creative action!

Your own questions will serve you best during Data-Finding. But the sample list on the following page should be helpful in giving you some ideas to help you get started. After you've read these questions, read the short passage that follows ("Printer's Ink") and practice some Data-Finding using the five W's and an H.

Printer's Ink

You work for a local business that does small job printing, binding, and production of custom paper products (note pads, etc.). There are about 25 people employed here, including yourself. Each year, the shop closes for one week, so the employees can catch up on back orders, take care of paperwork and maintenance, and have some time to work without the usual pressures associated with the daily flow of customers. Officially, this is a time for inventory, annual accounting, and equipment maintenance. There's plenty to do, but it can be done at a little less hectic pace than usual.

Within the organization there are press and machine operators, sales representatives and clerks, office personnel, and a small administrative staff.

This year, the President of the company (who is the owner) has decided to take advantage of the week to schedule a special 2½ day training program. He has hired a consulting firm to observe the organization and personnel and then develop a training program. He says that he wants to see increased sales, increased productivity, increased profits, and increased motivation. He wants results from the training program–but he also wants to be certain that, in the remaining part of the week, the jobs usually done during the "shut down week" will be completed. He's spending quite a bit of money on the training program and he says, "That's okay. My staff is worth every dollar of it!"

Try to put yourself into this situation. What Data-Finding can you do about this Mess? Use the 5 W's and H, and the sample questions. List your data on a separate sheet (or sheets!) of paper. Quite often, by the way, it is helpful to number each item on your list, making it easier to use the data later.

What do you know? What information do you have? What impressions have you formed? What observations have you made? What feelings or hunches do you have?

What else do you *need* to know? Is there some "must" information you need? What else would you *like* to know (even though it might not be critical or "must know" information)?

Data-Finding Questions About The Mess

Who are the important people involved? From Where? Why are they important? Why are they involved? How?

Who are the other people that are involved? Why are they involved? How? Where are they from?

What groups are involved? How are they involved? Where are they from? Why are these groups involved?

Who has special strengths or resources that are a part of this Mess? What are these special strengths or resources? Why are they a part of the Mess?

Who might have information about this Mess that I don't have? How did they get it? From where? Why don't I have it?

Who might gain if this Mess is resolved? Why? How will they gain? When?

What rewards or incentives are available to me in this Mess? From where? How are they available? From whom?

What standards or requirements must I satisfy in dealing with this Mess? Why? Who set them? When?

What advantages exist for solving this Mess? Why are they advantages?

What disadvantages exist for solving this Mess? Why are they disadvantages?

What difficulties can I anticipate in this Mess? Why are they difficulties? How have these difficulties been dealt with in the past? By whom? Where?

What success have I achieved so far with this Mess? How? Why? When?

What can I do to insure success with this Mess? How? Why? When?

What times are involved in this Mess? Hours, days, dates? Why?

What places are involved in this Mess? Locations? How? Why?

What parts of this Mess provide opportunities or challenges? Why? How?

What parts of this Mess could be considered a crisis? Why? How?

What influence do I have over people, places, resources and times that are involved in this Mess? Why?

What does this Mess look, smell, feel, taste and sound like? Why?

What is my gut feeling about this Mess? Why?

How are my feelings influencing my behavior? Am I excited? Enthusiastic? Am I anxious? Apprehensive? Why?

How did this Mess happen or develop? When? Where? Why?

How have I tried to deal with this Mess? When? Why?

How do others see this Mess? Who? Why?

How is their view similar to or different from mine? Why?

Creative Problem Solving: The Basic Course

DDF-7: HI-TECH HELPERS

If you own or use regularly a personal or home computer, this exercise is for you. If you haven't entered the wonderful world of high technology yet, feel free to proceed directly to the next exercise.

Computers can help us in a variety of ways. They won't solve our problems for us, but they can be valuable tools in storing, organizing, and recalling lots of information quickly and efficiently. Here are some preliminary questions we hope will be useful by suggesting some productive problem solving applications for your computer:

1. How can your WORD PROCESSING program be helpful in Data-Finding?
2. Do you have a "SPREAD-SHEET" or accounting program? If so, what does it help you to do with DATA? How can this be used in Data-Finding in CPS?
3. Do you have a program for filing, organizing your calendar, or scheduling the steps of a project? How can you see these programs to help you in Data-Finding?
4. Some powerful software involves creating and using "data bases." If you are familiar with one or more of these programs, how can you use it to best advantage in Data-Finding for a Mess?
5. Can you write programs of your own for your computer (in a language such as BASIC, for example)? What kinds might be useful in Data-Finding?
6. Can you create graphs, charts, or graphics with your computer or printer? If so, how do these capabilities extend or enhance your ability to gather, organize, or analyze data about a Mess?
7. Do you have a modem? What is the impact of high-speed, computer-to-computer communication and networking on our Data-Finding efforts?

HOW MUCH DATA DO YOU NEED?
WHEN DO YOU HAVE "ENOUGH DATA?"

The divergent phase of Data-Finding can be interesting and stimulating. Your problem solving will improve as you develop your proficiency in searching for information, ideas, and alternatives. But you also have to learn how to be effective in sifting through the data, sorting out the pieces, and locating the most important or promising components on which to build your later efforts. That's what we describe as the convergent phase.

In some ways, you might think you can never have "enough" data–that new piece of information, just around the corner, might be the real "clincher," or the critical bit of information that will cause everything else to fall neatly into place. It's good to remember that, as long as it doesn't become counter-productive. Don't become so fascinated with the diverging and with thinking about what *might* yet turn up that you *never* bring yourself to the point of converging and making choices.

You'll realize that it's time to begin the converging process when you find that some of the data begin to "jump out at you." After you've stretched and looked at the Mess from many different points of view, certain observations and information will begin to take on special significance. You may begin to recognize these by being alert to the feeling that says, "Oh, yes, of course–I need to keep that one in mind; it's really important!"

Converging Activities

Let's try some exercises to help you learn how to proceed effectively and deliberately in the converging phase of Data-Finding.

CDF-1: D-F DECISION GUIDELINES

You can use several guidelines to determine when it's time to begin "converging." These are informal "tests" to use in your decision-making, not hard-and-fast "rules."

You can tell that you have enough data when . . . .

1. . . . . you find your attention starting to shift to intriguing questions and problem statements, rather than listing more data;
2. . . . . you can "spot" several areas that seem to cluster around a common area of concern or needed information and ideas;
3. . . . . you can forecast or project several topics that are important for you to pursue;
4. . . . . one AHA! hits you . . . . some of the data just seem to "jump out at you" and demand attention. We call this an "Interocular test" because the data "leap up and hit you between the eyes." (but, *be sure to stretch!*)
5. . . . . you have a very extensive list of data, including many "obvious" pieces of information and several new or unusual perceptions or observations, and you've already completed several cycles of active data generation (you've felt as if you were "running out of gas" at least once before and then found a second "burst" of ideas). We have found the idea of extended effort to be fruitful in each divergent stage of CPS, but especially during the Data-Finding stage. Look over the list of data you generated for "Printer's Ink" and see how these guidelines might be applied.

Creative Problem Solving: The Basic Course

CDF-2: HITS, HOT SPOTS, AND RELATES

Take your list of data from Exercise DDF-6 (in which you worked on the "Printer's Ink" Mess) and look through it. Place an asterisk or check mark next to any items that seem to represent particularly important items or areas. Among all the data you recorded, do some items seem to warrant closer attention? Are some matters you believe to be especially important? Do they seem to describe the "heart" or the "essence" of the situation? Those are the items that you should mark; we call them, "Hits."

Write down the numbers of the items you considered "Hits" for your data list from the "Printer's Ink" Mess:

_____   _____

_____   _____

Do some of the "Hits" deal with the same general subject or aspect of the Mess? If so, group them together, to form clusters of ideas. These clusters are called, "Hot Spots." They are segments of data that represent "hot" issues–significant issues that will demand your attention when working on the Mess.

Regroup your list of "Hits" to bring one or more clusters or "Hot Spots" together. Use the left column in the chart below:

HOT SPOTS List items:	RELATIONSHIP: How are these items related to each other?
_____	_____
_____	_____
_____	_____

Use extra pages for additional Hot Spots.

If you have difficulty finding clusters among the Hits, you might try this approach:

1. Enter the first "Hit" from your list in Box A in the chart below.
2. Take the second "Hit" from your list. Does it deal with the same subject or area as the first one? If so, put its number in Box A. If not, put it in Box B.
3. Take the third "Hit" from your list. If it deals with the same theme or area as the *first* Hit, put its number in Box A; if it's the same as the *second* Hit, put it in Box B; if it's a *new* one, use the next box.
4. Continue as in Step 3 for each item on your list of "Hits."
   Now, inspect each box in the chart (these are the clusters or "Hot Spots"). How are the items in each box related?

A	B	C
D	E	F
G	H	I
J	K	L

60

Creative Problem Solving: The Basic Course

CDF-3: CRITICAL CONCERNS

It's early April and there's quite a bit for you to be concerned about in your little fishing bait and tackle shop. The trout season has just opened, and there have been lots of people who wanted to renew their state fishing licenses. Everybody seems to remember that at the last minute. They also want to know if there have been any changes in the law this year: How big must the Rainbow Trout be to keep? How many can we keep in a day? etc. And, of course, they also want to know where to find the biggest and easiest-to-catch fish. What baits are the best ones to use? In addition, now that the ice is out, it's time to be thinking about putting out the docks, replacing the worn anchor ropes on the rental rowboats, checking the inventory of life jackets and cushions, and generally preparing for the steady flow of boat renters from now until November. Are the boat registrations all current? Did we repair the leaky boats? Replace the broken oars?

While all this is racing through your mind, a friend reminds you that it's almost Income Tax time. (With friends like that, who needs enemies?) You find yourself starting to wonder where you put that big box full of last year's receipts. The people from the Health Department and the Department of Environmental Conservation will probably also be here any day now to check the water supply and various licenses and permits. Then you remember that you were going to write a classified advertisement for the local "Pennysaver" because you want to hire a new weekend clerk. You were also supposed to return the call from the Chamber of Commerce about renewing your membership and taking out an ad in this summer's Visitor's Information Guide.

Using this typical springtime scenario, practice some Data-Finding, and make a numbered data list. Then, put yourself in the place of the manager/owner of the shop, go through the list and identify some of the most important data (the "Hits"). Identify some Hot Spots, and consider what they have in common ("Relates").

The next step is to begin to determine which clusters represent the "Critical Concerns." Which ones do you believe should receive the most attention? Which ones should be considered first? What factors influence your decisions?

This step in converging is important because it helps you to be certain that you are using your real priorities and concerns in searching for possible problem statements. Look carefully and critically at *all* the data you've gathered, to determine which areas hold the greatest *need* and *promise* for developing specific problem statements.

For this Mess, use your own data list and your chart of Hits and Hot Spots to establish some priorities:

HOT SPOT	PRIORITY ASSIGNED	REASONS/JUSTIFICATION
_____	____ High - Immediate Attention	_____
	____ Medium - Act Soon	_____
	____ Low - "Back Burner"	_____
_____	____ High ____ Medium ____ Low	_____
		_____
		_____
_____	____ High ____ Medium ____ Low	_____
		_____

Creative Problem Solving: The Basic Course

_____   ___High   ___Medium   ___Low   _____

_____

_____

_____   ___High   ___Medium   ___Low   _____

_____

_____

Your "High" priority represent "Critical Concern" areas. These might be your first priorities to consider as you begin the next CPS stage (Problem-Finding).

CDF-4: MUST, NEED, & LIKE TO KNOW

Some people enjoy shopping for a new car; others consider it a difficult or even painful task. If you've ever gone through this process, you know that it can present a great variety of choices and often some that are very difficult. Let's look at a fairly typical case.

The New Car

As Carol entered the showroom, her eyes wandered from one glittering machine to another. Every car on the floor looked beautiful; how would she ever choose? Momentarily, her gaze settled on a beautiful metallic silver convertible in the center of the showroom, its top down, inviting the feel of the cool breeze on a bright sunny day. The interior was handcrafted leather, elegant and luxurious. "I'll bet it has every option they can put on it," thought Carol as she walked toward the convertible, and sure enough it did. The base price was about $12,000, but the total price was almost $17,000. It had everything–power windows, power door locks, special tires and wire wheels, a super-deluxe stereo and tape deck, air conditioning, and lots of extra "creature comforts." She glanced at the efficiency rating on the window sticker: mileage estimate–14 miles per gallon of gas. Power in reserve to pass anything except a gas station, and gas is *so* expensive! But then her thoughts drifted to the exhilerating feeling of gliding along a highway by the coast, top down, hair blowing in the breeze, sea air fresh in the early morning–a day just made for a silver convertible.

Seventeen thousand dollars is quite a lot of money–a good part of a year's salary, even for an experienced teacher, thought Carol. Let's see, even at the present rates of the Credit Union, with about $5,000 down payment and trade-in allowance, what would the payments be? (Later, the salesman looked in his secret little green book–the payments would "only" be about $275.00 a month. "Only!")

She couldn't resist taking the convertible out for a test drive, just to see how it felt. It did feel great, but she knew it would; it was so much more fun than her five year old sedan with the broken radio. It did make a lot of noise, though, and it rattled more than any sedan ever would on the bumpy road. Even with the top up, the wind noise was substantial. You'd have to get used to that. There wasn't much of a back seat, which might make it difficult for the car pool. When she returned to the dealer's lot, she looked in the rear deck, and she was surprised. The deep well for the top and the mechanism that raised and lowered it took up a great deal of space; you would have to be clever to store more than a small suitcase in that space. Eventually, Carol decided to buy a very pretty blue sport sedan. It was several thousand dollars less expensive, and it had much more room as well as a much more economical engine.

Let's consider the Data-Finding that Carol might have done as she considered her new car purchase. Can you determine how Carol might have classified data into these three categories:

What were the V.I.D. ("Very Important Data")?

> These are data that *must* be considered in dealing effectively with the Mess.
> The V.I.D. are the data Carol *had* to consider in making her final decision.

What were some data that Carol considered as "like to have" or "want to have" in her car purchase?

> These are considerations that express desires or preferences, things that we'd *like* to consider, even though we may not *have* to consider them.

From the information given, you can probably make some reasonable inferences about Carol's analysis of the data. What data would you put in these categories:

Data Carol considered . . . .

Very Important Data (MUST Consider . . . .)	Preference Data (WANT or LIKE to Consider . . . .)

CDF-5: DATA-FINDING MATRIX

A Data-Finding Matrix can be very useful to you for examining a lengthy list. It will help you to organize and review the data systematically.

A sample of a Data-Finding Matrix appears below. It includes opportunities for you to "collect" and "sort" your data using several of the techniques you have practiced in the previous divergent and convergent Data-Finding exercises. It can also be used in combination with any of the other kinds of "worksheets" you have used in the specific exercises.

DATA-FINDING DIVERGING MATRIX

Brief Description of Mess:

	KNOW:	√VID	NEED/LIKE TO KNOW:	√VID
WHO				
WHAT				
WHERE				
WHEN				
WHY				
HOW				

CPF-6: DATA-FINDING CONVERGING MATRIX

A. Search D-F Diverging Matrix For Very Important Data (√VID)

DATA "HOT SPOTS"		
Know:	Need to Know:	Like to Know:

B. What Common Dimensions ("Themes") Can Be Found In Section A.? ➡ What Major Areas To Investigate Do These Represent?

C. Highlight/Paraphrase–Essential Elements Of This Situation:

CHAPTER 5

Problem-Finding: Structuring the Problem

> **Problem-Finding Stage**
>
> Many possible statements of problems and subproblems are generated. The most appropriate problem statement(s) is chosen.

After studying this chapter, you will be able to:

1. Define and give examples of essential elements of problem statements.
2. Generate many different problem statements for a given situation.
3. Combine problem statements based on common elements.
4. Select productive problem statements based upon the application of specific guidelines.
5. Broaden and redefine problem statements by using different levels of abstraction, changing key words and identifying subproblems.
6. Choose, select and evaluate from among a variety of possible problem statements, those which offer the greatest potential for productive Idea-Finding.

Problem-Finding: Structuring the Problem

As you have already seen, creative problem solving is a general system designed to help you solve a wide variety of problems. In Mess-Finding you identified many situations on which you may have considered working. Then, you prioritized and evaluated these messes to ensure ownership and outlook. After selecting a particular mess on which to work, you became involved in Data-Finding to analyze many different aspects of your Mess. Converging during Data-Finding provided you with information about the most important and promising aspects of your Mess for continued investigation.

In the Problem-Finding stage you will search for a number of more specific questions or "problem statements" about which you wish to find some new and useful ideas. The convergent phase of Problem-Finding will lead to a problem statement which describes the problem in a way that you consider most effective and important in guiding your Idea-Finding.

In a sense, the first three stages of CPS have in common the "search for a fertile view of the situation." Even though you are dealing with situations and challenges in Mess-Finding and information, feelings, and questions in Data-Finding, the general outcome of these stages is to establish an adequate foundation for productive Problem-Finding. During Problem-Finding the result of all your previous problem-solving energy comes to a decision point, which will channel and direct your energies for the remaining stages of the process.

Problem definition is not a simple, mechanical activity. By virtue of what you do during CPS, you must use your imagination by inventing a definition of the problem. Some people mistakenly use the word "problem" to describe situations in which only simple recall and mechanical thinking are necessary. These are often simple puzzles, "brainteasers" or "word problems" that call for the application of a specific formula (a pattern or algorithm) in every instance. For example, in a math class you were probably taught that the area of a rectangle is side A multiplied by side B. You were then given the length of side A and side B of some rectangle and asked to find the Area. Although this might have been called a problem, it really involves only the routine recall and use of the formula. The mental abilities needed in this activity were largely only memory and recall. In additiion, for most such problems, only *one* answer is acceptable. This single correct answer is usually already known to others but needs to be determined by the "problem solver."

While knowledge, recall and convergent production are important aspects of thinking and learning, the primary value of CPS is its use in solving problems that require imagination, generation of knowledge, and open-ended thinking. Thus CPS goes beyond convergent, puzzle-type problems which are presented in "ready to solve" fashion. In fact, the most fruitful uses of CPS are for problem situations which allow for your own, personal interest, influence and imagination. These situations, which are very important to you, provide opportunities to generate or discover new and productive courses of action. You actually need to formulate an original and useful definition of the problem. There is no single correct answer that you are simply trying to discover. You can't look up the answer to a real CPS problem "in the back of the book!" You may need to break away from common views of the problem, and you must feel free to diverge, to use your senses, and to create new perspectives about the situation. Achieving this perspective may be facilitated by Mess-Finding and Data-Finding, but the important function of Problem-Finding is stating the challenge so you can focus on searching for a variety of alternatives.

Certainly there is no shortage of problems within each Mess. They are all around us. But the knowledge that they exist isn't sufficient in itself to insure that they can be recognized and solved. As Getzels (1975) indicated, problems "must be posed and formulated in fruitful and often radical ways if they are to be moved toward solution (p. 12)." Posing and formulating problem statements are key activities during Problem-Finding.

The importance of developing a statement which reflects the "real" problem cannot be overstated. This ability is a part of the creativity of the artist (see Getzels and Csikszentmihalyi, 1976) as well as for the scientist. In discussing the development of physics, Einstein and Infeld (1938) asserted:

The formulation of a problem is often more important than its solution, which may be merely a

Creative Problem Solving: The Basic Course

matter of mathematical or experimental skill. To raise new questions, new possibilities, to regard old problems from a new angle, requires imagination and marks real advance in science.

Stating the problem

As John Dewey stated, *"A problem is half-solved if properly stated."* We see a problem statement as a question about which you, as the owner of the problem, want to gather ideas. To select the "best" statement of the problem, it is important first to diverge and be certain you have some options which provide several different perspectives on your problem situation.

It will be helpful to state the problem in a particular way. We use the phrase "In what ways might (IWWM) . . ." or "How to (H_2) . . ." to start each problem statement. We call this the *invitational stem*. This kind of phrase allows room for uncertainty and helps avoid the trap of premature convergence by settling on *one* statement which remains within only *one* perception of the mess. (Having only a single view may actually be the reason it is important to deal with your Mess in the first place!)

The other ingredients of a CPS problem statement are *ownership* and *action*. An effective statement identifies *who* might do *what*. When generating many statements, it is helpful to examine a number of different aspects of ownership as well as a wide variety of possible actions. For example, read the newspaper article "Inmate is giant of problem" and write your initial problem statement (Yes, really write it out!).

Inmate Is Giant Of Problem

NEW YORK (UPI) — A giant inmate who prison guards claim can break his handcuffs at will has Rikers Island prison in a state of terror, a spokesman for the guards' union said Friday.

Correction officials admitted that they don't know what to do with Vernon Williams, who stands 6-foot-3 and weighs 375 pounds.

Williams, who is in jail waiting trial for four different charges, including assault and robbery, has been charged with assaulting six prison officials and two nurses during his stay at Rikers Island.

After Williams was charged with assaulting the nurses in October, prison officials ordered that he be handcuffed whenever leaving his cell, and accompanied at all times by no fewer than five guards.

"It would be funny if it wasn't so serious," said one corrections official.

On Friday, Williams allegedly attacked officer Jose Aponte, breaking his nose.

After that incident, Phil Seelig, president of the Corrections Officers Benevolent Association, announced that his men would not go near Williams any longer.

Reprinted by permission of UPI.

Use data from the article to write your initial statement:

IWWM_____

_____

_____

_____

_____

_____

_____

Use your statement as a basis for comparing the general suggestions in the remaining pages of this chapter.

First, check to see that you have identified *someone* who will do *something*. An example would be: "In what ways might the guards control Vernon?" This statement identifies the guards as having ownership over the activity of controlling Vernon. Does your statement have a similar perception of the Mess? The action part of the problem statement actually includes an action verb and a goal or area (objective) of concern. In the example, the action verb is *control* and *Vernon* is the object of concern. The figure below illustrates the basic elements of a problem statement for CPS. We have used the problem statement: "IWWM the guards control Vernon?" for the example:

COMPONENTS OF A PROBLEM STATEMENT

IN WHAT WAYS MIGHT (HOW MIGHT)	THE GUARDS	CONTROL	VERNON?
INVITATIONAL STEM	OWNER	ACTION VERB	GOAL OR AREA OF OBJECTIVE/CONCERN

Another aspect to check for is the existence of criteria. Does your statement include things that will decrease your ability to find ideas? An example would be a statement like: "In what ways might the guards control Vernon so he doesn't hurt himself or others and in such a way so that it doesn't cost very much?" This statement includes all sorts of limitations for your Idea-Finding efforts. Limitations such as cost and effect on Vernon or others may be very important to consider, but not at *this* stage of the process. In *Solution-Finding* you will be able to generate many limiting factors to use in judging and evaluating *all* your ideas. Keep in mind that now, during Problem-Finding, you are simply concerned with defining the problem in ways that will help you gather ideas. It is crucial to *diverge* during Problem-Finding to be certain to uncover some new, interesting and more fruitful definitions of the problem.

Another reason why you shouldn't worry about including many constraints or limitations within the problem statement is that you will also have the opportunity to converge during Problem-Finding. After generating a wide variety of optional problem statements you will have to select one (or a few) which reflect(s) the best possible avenues for generating ideas. If you produced a few wild and crazy statements, the chances are better that you have stretched your thinking to produce new and useful perspectives on your situation.

Once certain that your statement includes ownership and action and avoids limiting words, you are ready to examine another element in developing an effective problem statement: *brevity*. Does your statement ramble in describing the situation that would satisfy the question? Although we cannot give you the exact number of words for all effective problem statements, we can tell you that it is best to be brief. For the example we have been studying (The Inmate Story), what do you think about this problem statement?

In what ways might the guards attempt to control Vernon as they are walking to and from the various buildings of the prison which requires that they keep him handcuffed and which results in Vernon behaving in a rather violent manner and causing harm to himself and to others?

This terrible problem statement would only promote confusion! It introduces so many things into one statement that it is difficult to recognize any specific or important area of concern. Generally, then, keep your statements short and to the point.

To assist you in remembering to be *brief* in stating problems, it might help to think of a newspaper headline. It's a concise, boldly-stated way of expressing an important thought. It gets right to the "heart" of the story. A well constructed problem-statement is in many ways similar to a "headline."

Although there are many ways to find or develop problem statements, an effective starting point is the list of information, ideas, and questions that you developed in the Data-Finding stage. The important part of Data-Finding (especially in the Convergent Phase) was to help you identify the most significant aspects of your Mess. Very often, the "hot spots" from your Data-Finding list will be extremely useful in Problem-Finding because you can translate them directly into IWWM . . . or H_2 questions. Many of the "Need and Want to know" aspects of Data-Finding can also become questions or problem statements through simple wording changes.

Diverging Activities

Now that you have examined the basic elements of a problem statement you are ready to practice developing a large pool of possible statements. The importance of this phase was supported by Wertheimer (1959) when he stated:

The function of thinking is not just solving an actual problem but discovering, envisaging, going into deeper questions. Often in great discoveries the most important thing is that a certain question is found. Envisaging, putting the productive question is often more important, often a greater achievement than solution of a set question.

The divergent phase of Problem-Finding results in a broad collection of viewpoints toward the situation at hand. A variety of techniques will be useful in developing these statements. Some techniques provide you many variations on a similar "theme;" others will help you to examine deliberately several different avenues or directions for problem solving.

DPF-1: LISTING OWNERSHIP AND ACTION ELEMENTS

Let's go back to the example of Vernon, the convict. Use your understanding of the situation to generate *at least* ten different people or groups who might have an element of ownership in the Mess (for example: guards, Vernon, etc.):

1. _____
2. _____
3. _____
4. _____
5. _____
6. _____
7. _____
8. _____
9. _____
10. _____

Now, identify *at least* ten types of actions which might be considered for the situation (for example: control, protect, etc.):

1. _____
2. _____
3. _____
4. _____
5. _____
6. _____
7. _____
8. _____
9. _____
10. _____

How do yours compare with those on the following page?

OWNERSHIP	ACTIONS
guards	control
nurses	handcuff
warden	buy stronger handcuffs
the local community	make stronger handcuffs
prisoners	subdue
Vernon	channel his energy
the State	improve prison life
Vernon's mom	feel protected
the guards' families	make himself useful
handcuff manufacturers	protect guards
	release him
	get him transferred

Also compare these elements of ownership and action with the first statement you developed on page 70 in this chapter. Are there any similarities? Do you notice any different or more productive alternatives?

Many individuals stay within certain boundaries when attempting to solve a problem. Sometimes, by simply brainstorming elements of ownership and action it is possible to come upon a new and more productive perspective.

In this example, Vernon really did create a "giant" of a problem for prison officials. In real life they generally remained within one definition of the problem which was a variation of "IWWM Vernon be controlled?" The prison officials spent a great deal of money and energy on this problem. Most of their resources went into trying to find better handcuffs. This unproductive search was abandoned only after they examined a new line of thinking. They discovered that Vernon had a very strong aversion to being handcuffed. He was not by nature an extremely violent person, but only reacted strongly when forced to wear handcuffs. When the prison officials identified this problem: "IWWMW channel Vernon's energies?" they eventually found a way to solve the "real" problem. They made Vernon responsible for the behavior of some peers. By making him a trustee, they channeled his energy and eliminated the need for handcuffs in the first place.

This may not be an earthshaking example, but you can see that many times people spend vast resources solving the "wrong" problem. How many examples can you think of where all that was necessary was some redefinition of the situation, or a change in perspective?

The purpose of diverging during this phase is to increase the likelihood that you can discover a productive definition for your situation. The technique you just used generated ten different elements of ownership and ten different actions. This produced a total possible pool of (10 x 10) or 100 different problem definitions!

DPF-2: KEY WORD VARIATIONS

Another way to come up with a wide variety of problem statements is to use synonyms or substitutes for the key words in the statement. This technique is called "Key Word Variations." The first step is to examine a particular problem statement and identify the important or key words within it. For example, let's take a statement from our previous example:

"In what ways might we channel Vernon's energy?" Two key words in this statement are "channel" and "energy." Try brainstorming other words to substitute for each of these words:

CHANNEL

1. _____
2. _____
3. _____
4. _____
5. _____
6. _____
7. _____
8. _____
9. _____
10. _____

ENERGY

1. _____
2. _____
3. _____
4. _____
5. _____
6. _____
7. _____
8. _____
9. _____
10. _____

> Were you able to identify a more productive choice of words from the list you created? Many times, this technique results in the problem-solver selecting new words which provide a better expression of what is viewed to be the "real" problem.

The most productive word to change in the statement of the challenge is often the verb. Changing the verb may help you alter your mental "set" about the challenge. See the "Action Checklist" for a list of useful verbs for a variety of problem statements.

ACTION CHECKLIST

organize	appreciate	enrich	satisfy
arrange	admire	motivate	appease
assemble	enjoy	encourage	gratify
prepare	grateful	provoke	extend
order	approach	inspire	supply
distribute	converge	renew	grow from
systematize	plan	revive	learn from
schedule	change	refresh	experience
settle	modify	restore	increase
group	adapt	reward	amplify
develop	alter	improve	build
generate	exchange	amend	enlarge
produce	substitute	upgrade	enhance
evolve	switch	begin	magnify
disclose	endeavor	start	expand
express	strive	establish	perform
achieve	attempt	commence	manage
become	accomplish	originate	handle
mature	invent	initiate	conduct
grow	convey	launch	control

This technique is most useful in producing many variations on one particular point of view toward the challenge. When it is necessary to come up with a deliberate and totally different perception, use of other Problem-Finding techniques can also be helpful.

DPF-3: THE THREE LITTLE PIGS

As children, most of us have read the story of the "Three Little Pigs." Take a moment to recall the basic ideas of the story.

What are some problem statements that might be developed by someone within the story?

List your ideas here:

IWWM _____

_____

_____

_____

_____

_____

_____

Many groups with whom we have used this activity have suggested problem statements like these:

In what ways might the pigs build better homes?
IWWM the pigs find stronger materials to use?
IWWM the pigs keep the wolf away?
IWWM the pigs eliminate the wolf?
IWWM the pigs befriend the wolf?

Did you think of any others? Did you also remember that there are other characters in the story who might be able to state some problems? How about the wolf, for example? What might be some problems *from the wolf's viewpoint?*

IWWMI improve my huffing and puffing?
IWWMI catch the pigs when they're not in the house?
IWWMI get into the pigs' houses?
IWWMI reduce my desire for bacon?
IWWMI create a trap for the pigs?

Would anyone else look at the story differently, and thus identify *other* problems?

Police: IWWMW protect the pigs?
              IWWMW catch the wolf in the act?

Salesman: IWWMI sell more wolf traps?
              IWWMI lure the wolf to my meat market?
              IWWMI sell some powerful fans?

For any situation, don't forget to look for *many* different problem statements!

DPF-4: USING THE ABSTRACTION LADDER TO BROADEN OR NARROW PROBLEM STATEMENTS

Sometimes people frame their problem statements in very general or global terms. At other times the problem statement is too narrow or specific. Either way, the problem-solver appears to be working at an inappropriate level of abstraction.

More than 2,000 years ago Aristotle considered the concept of ends versus means. According to him, the ultimate end all people should pursue is a "good life." We can borrow from his thinking, and point out that the broadest possible problem statement anyone can consider is: "In what ways might I lead a richer, fuller life?" This is the ultimate "top of the abstraction ladder" or the end for all means, at least from a philosophical viewpoint.

Let's examine a specific example of why this abstraction ladder is so important in Problem-Finding. In this case, a second grade student named Johnny ran into a classroom, saw the teacher, and declared: "I've got to get a ladder!" The teacher asked, "What's your problem?" Johnny replied "I've got to get a ladder!"

At that point, Johnny was searching for a solution, and probably thought the teacher was hard of hearing. In fact, the teacher was trying to help. In this case the stated end for Johnny was "having the ladder." The teacher asked the important question: "Johnny, *why* do you need the ladder?" Johnny responded: "I've got to get my project off the top shelf of the bookcase." With that statement, Johnny's eyes lit up and off he went. He had evidently changed his viewpoint and redefined the problem. His stated end was really a means to another end.

When Johnny started out, he had only one possibility that would fit his definition of the problem. In this case, only finding a ladder would do. However, after moving one level up on the ladder of abstraction, he defined his problem as getting the project off the top shelf. For this problem he had quite a few more options which would fit his definition. In fact, he must have made a new connection as soon as he redefined the problem because we know he solved it. His eyes lit up and he left the room in a hurry. Later he was seen with his project. We don't know *how* he solved his problem, but he did–after he was able to state it effectively for himself.

Asking the question "Why?" or "What is my basic objective or reason for attempting this?" can help you reach a more adequate recognition of a challenge. The answers to these questions will usually provide the foundation for a new and more basic problem statement.

Let's really stretch the example provided by our second grader. Johnny recognized his more appropriate placement on the ladder of abstraction and immediately put his plan into action. To illustrate how far we could go by using the broadening technique of asking "why?", refer to Figure V-1. Start with the second rung on the ladder, where Johnny has already redefined his first statement by examining the question "IWWMI get my project off the top shelf?" The second time the question "Why?" might have been asked would have resulted in the redefinition "IWWMI get a good grade in social studies?" The teacher could have continued the process of asking "Why?" until, eventually, they reached the top.

Of course, we are not recommending doing this each time you wish to redefine a problem. We hope this illustrates that there is a ladder which has at the very top the "search for happiness." Johnny got off the ladder when he reached a more appropriate level of abstraction. The owner of any problem can use this ladder to broaden the definition of the situation and then select a statement which provides a better viewpoint from which to gather ideas.

Figure V-1.

TEACHER	PROBLEM STATEMENT	JOHNNY
Oh!	IWWMI lead a richer, fuller life?	I need a good job so that I can lead a happy life.
	WHY?	
Why do you want to get a good job when you grow up?	IWWMI ensure that I have a good career?	Because I want to be able to get a good job when I grow up.
	WHY?	
Why do you wnat to do well in school?	IWWMI do well in school?	Because I want to do well in school.
	WHY?	
Why do you want a good grade in Social Studies?	IWWMI get a good grade in Social Studies?	I want to get a good grade in my Social Studies class.
	WHY?	
Why do you need to get your project off the top shelf?	IWWMI get my project off the top shelf?	Because I need to get my project off the top shelf of the bookcase.
	WHY?	
Why do you need a ladder?	IWWMI get a ladder?	I've got to get a ladder!

Creative Problem Solving: The Basic Course

> Knowing what you are looking for helps you to recognize it when you see it. But in the case of innovation, how do you know what you are looking for? You don't unless you state your problem so broadly, so basically, so all inclusively and generically, that you do not preclude even the remotest possibilities—so that you do not pre-condition your mind to a narrow range of acceptable answers.
>
> *John E. Arnold,*
> Professor of Engineering

Select a challenge you are familiar with and for which you have some degree of ownership. Use our special preface to actually develop a Problem-Finding statement:

Initial Statement: _____

_____

Now, restate the problem using the "Why?" technique to broaden your viewpoint. Stop when you get to the richer, fuller life:

Restatement 1 _____

Restatement 2 _____

Restatement 3 _____

Restatement 4 _____

Restatement 5 _____

Restatement 6 _____

Restatement 7 _____

Restatement 8 _____

Restatement 9 _____

Restatement 10 _____

You just focused on using the abstraction ladder to broaden the statement of the problem. You can also use this concept in reverse, to break down a general problem statement.

Many times, when people are asked to identify a challenge for CPS they remain general or stay fairly high on the abstraction ladder. For example, let's take Bob who selects the messy area of personal health. He generates lots of data and selects the following as key facts to consider:

1. I am forty pounds overweight.
2. I don't feel healthy.
3. I don't have time to exercise.
4. I live alone.
5. I am not eating right.

Bob says that he knows what his problem is and that he has always known what it has been: "I need to feel more healthy!" It ought to be clear by now that this viewpoint is pretty high on the abstraction ladder. Let's teach Bob how to bring the problem down a few rungs.

1. First, remind him to use "IWWMI . . ." and that we are looking for a statement to help him generate some ideas.

2. Next, let's ask him *"How* would you feel more healthy?" or *"What's preventing you* from feeling healthy now?" He might respond "IWWMI lose some weight?"

3. One more rung: *"How* might you lose some weight?" or *"What's* preventing you from losing weight right now?" He might respond "IWWMI develop a plan to lose weight?"

By asking the questions "How?" or "What's preventing you from . . . ?" you can bring yourself down the ladder of abstraction. Simply paraphrase your response to the questions and restate them using IWWM . . .

Another way to view this situation may be helpful in breaking it down into smaller elements.

SUBPROBLEM:
IWWMI find time to exercise?

SUBPROBLEM:
IWWMI develop a plan to lose weight?

SUBPROBLEM:
IWWMI motivate myself to keep to my plan?

SUBPROBLEM:
List other subproblems . . .

This figure illustrates that it can be useful to break down a general statement into its smaller units. These subproblems may be more fruitful for you to gather some ideas. They allow you to focus your Idea-Finding efforts. Choose one of these to work on because it describes the most important subproblem for you. Another option is to gather ideas systematically for each subproblem. In this example, it may be most important for Bob to find ideas to motivate himself to keep to his plan. In this case, he might examine this subproblem after developing a plan.

Breaking the fuzzy and general statement down into smaller elements provides you some additional and perhaps more targeted choices from which to choose.

Start off with the broadest Problem-Finding statement: "IWWMI lead a rich, full life?" and practice going down the ladder of abstraction. Stop when you get to where you really want to gather some ideas:

Restatement 1 _____

Restatement 2 _____

Restatement 3 _____

Restatement 4 _____

Restatement 5 _____

Restatement 6 _____

Restatement 7 _____

Restatement 8 _____

Restatement 9 _____

Restatement 10 _____

DPF-5: WHY ELSE? OR HOW ELSE?

When traveling up or down the abstraction ladder you may only provide a single response to the question posed. In the example, Johnny told us only one reason why he wanted the ladder. Realistically, there may be many situations where it is possible to remain at a particular rung on the ladder and provide a number of different responses.

For the health example, you might have begun with an assertion like: "I have to lose weight!" The problem statement would read: "IWWMI lose weight?" If you asked yourself "Why do I want to lose weight?" you might initially respond that "I want to feel more healthy." Staying at this level of abstraction, you could then ask: *"Why else* do I want to lose weight?" Another possible response could be "I want to fit my clothes again!" This could be converted into a related problem statement like: "IWWMI update my wardrobe?"

It is possible to continue diverging during Problem-Finding until you find a statement on which you really want to work. You could ask "Why else?" (for going up the ladder) or "How else?" (for when you're on your way down) until you hit something that triggers a feeling that you really want to collect ideas on that area. Sometimes, you may want to use some incubation time (putting the problem in the back of your mind for awhile) before concluding the search for a view of the problem on which to gather options.

Now, search your experiences for a situation that called for you to actually redefine the view you had of the problem in order to produce some fruitful alternatives. What was your original view?

IWWMI_____

_____

_____

Your redefinition: IWWMI_____

_____

_____

Use the "Why or How else?" technique to generate five other ways you could have viewed the situation.

1._____

2._____

3._____

4._____

5._____

Converging Activities

There is no magic way to know when to stop generating possible problem statements and begin converging. We cannot tell you that after generating 26 problem statements it is time to decide which ones you will use for Idea-Finding for *all* problem situations. Generally, the problem's owner provides the decision-making about how far to go during the divergent phase. When you recognize plenty of useful avenues as a result of your Problem-Finding efforts, then it is time to begin convergence.

Convergence in Problem-Finding involves choosing the problem statement that seems to best capture the essence of the situation. This choice may appear to be most important or productive to consider at that point in time. This choosing and deciding provides the starting point for generating ideas, and thus, for solving the problem.

The use of convergent techniques provides you some "closure" to help you proceed to the following stages of CPS. Remember that your eventual aim is to develop a successful Plan of Action, which you are actually ready and willing to put to work. You do not "lose" any of the alternative Problem-Finding statements when you choose. Those not chosen at one point are still available for later consideration if you want them! The decisions you make during the convergent phase of Problem-Finding (as with all the other stages of CPS) should be viewed as tentative choices. Convergent techniques are tools to help you move through the process, not rigid rules forcing you to do things against your common sense or better judgment. In fact, the tools allow you to channel your common sense so it can be viewed and examined in the open. That way you can retrace your line of thinking and, if necessary, change it.

Creative Problem Solving: The Basic Course

CPF-1: HIGHLIGHTING

> NOTE: The first time this technique was written and published was in *The Handbook for Creative Learning* edited by Treffinger, Isaksen and Firestien. Much of the content describing this convergent technique has been taken from this source.

When you are attempting to select your most promising options during Problem-Finding, the use of the Highlighting procedure can be fruitful. The procedure consists of identifying "hits," "relates" and hotspots" and forming a restatement that refines your view of the situation.

A "hit" is a problem statement that strikes you as a breakthrough, aha, or direction to be pursued further. Hits are statements which provide insight or intrigue you and which could form the basis for a productive approach to gather ideas. Hits occur in Problem-Finding when a problem statement captures the essence of a situation or casts it in a new light.

After you identify a number of hits, "relates" are found. Finding relationships among identified hits is the key to this operation. Ask the question: "Which problem statements relate to each other?" Suppose you find two or three that seem to share a common relationship. These form a "hot spot." You may also find another group of statements that relate. In other words, you may identify more than one hot spot within a listing of possible problem statements for any challenge.

A "hot spot" is a collection of hits focusing on a specific issue or relating to similar aspects of the problem. It can also be a dominant idea, trend or theme. Hot spots provide raw material for restatements of the problem.

Once you have identified your hits and found the relationships among a particular group, you are ready to identify how that group relates. In a sense, you are providing a new statement combining the elements of agreement or a new label for the hot spot. This new version provides a more comprehensive translation and sets you up for productive Idea-Finding.

To help you use this converging technique, we have provided a transcript of a session led by a facilitator (a trained CPS group leader) in which highlighting was used. For this particular situation, the person who owned the problem (client) was John, a newspaper reporter who was dissatisfied with his assignment. He wanted to develop a strategy to move into another department at the paper.

The transcript below provides you a brainstormed list of 26 problem statements and the facilitator has asked John to identify the hits or problem statements for which he wanted to get some ideas. John then selected the hits and marked them with an asterisk.

```
 * 1. In what ways might I change the style of beat reporting?
 * 2. IWWMI get the financial beat accepted?
 * 3. IWWMI get recognized more professionally?
 * 4. IWWMI change the image of city hall reporting?
   5. IWWMI get back into suburban reporting?
   6. IWWMI bring ten cities to city hall?
   7. IWWMI make memos explosive?
   8. IWWMI win the Pulitzer?
 * 9. IWWMI build on reporting experience for leverage?
 *10. IWWMI use people I am in contact with daily to generate ideas?
 *11. IWWMI encourage dialogue of movement?
 *12. IWWMI talk to people on beat on ways to get out of beat?
  13. IWWMI get a lottery for this beat?
 *14. IWWMI convince others in management that other people's enthusiasm will better
      support the paper than my attitude?
 *15. IWWMI expand the city hall beat?
  16. IWWMI stay in touch and be out of the building?
 *17. IWWMI create a "get John back on the streets" campaign?
 *18. IWWMI use politics to my advantage?
  19. IWWMI get politicians on my campaign?
  20. IWWMI get unburied from the desk?
```

*21. IWWMI get their "monkey" off my back?
*22. IWWMI convey my feelings without playing the heavy?
*23. IWWMI resolve the image of being a "heavy?"
*24. IWWMI make city hall more descriptive?
*25. IWWMI create a win/win situation?
*26. IWWMI create an environment where concerns can be effectively communicated between parties?

To illustrate the *highlighting* procedure, we will use the following dialogue between the facilitator and the client.

Facilitator: "John, do you see some relationships or groupings among the problem statement you identified as hits? Which ones?"

John: "Let's see. Well 3, 9, and 14 relate; 10, 11, 12, and 17 relate; 1, 4, 15, and 24 relate; and 22, 23, 25, and 26 relate."

(The facilitator notes these four hot spots on a flipchart, leaving enough space between them to write John's *Paraphrase*.)

F: "OK, John, we have now isolated four hot spots. Would you say back to me what each hot spot represents to you in the form of a problem statement?"

J: "Well, 3, 9, and 14 would be to use my professional experience to my best advantage."

F: "Would you turn that into a problem statement for me?"

J: "Yes, Hmm, IWWMI use my professional experience to my best advantage?"

(Facilitator notes the paraphrased problem statement on the flipchart.)

F: "Good. Thanks. What about problem statements 10, 11, 12, and 17?"

J: "Yes, that would be IWWMI use the people I come in contact with daily as support for my concern?"

(Facilitator notes on flipchart.)

F: "Thanks. What about numbers 1, 4, 15, and 24?"

J: "OK . . . IWWMI make my present beat more interesting?"

(Facilitator notes on flipchart.)

F: "Finally, how about 22, 23, 25, and 26?"

J: "IWWMI communicate my concerns effectively to my editors to create a win/win situation?"

(Facilitator notes on flipchart.)

F: "Thank you, John. Of these four problem statements, would you say back to me the problem statement or combination of problem statements you would like to get some ideas for solving?"

J: "Well, I think the last one we came up with is the one I'd like to get some ideas on."

F: "Would you say that statement back to me?"

J: "Sure. IWWMI communicate my concerns effectively to my editors to create a win/win situation?"

(Facilitator lists on top of Idea-Finding page.)

F: "OK, group, what are all the ideas that you can possibly imagine to help John solve his problem: 'In what ways might I communicate my concerns effectively to my editors to create a win/win situation?'"

As you can see from this transcript, John did the convergent thinking by isolating the hits, determining which hits related to each other, forming ideas about the hot spots, and then condensing several related problem statements into one restatement. This procedure may create several clusters of related problem statements. It may be that you identify a few problem statements and choose to deal with each one for gathering ideas. However, you may be able to identify *one* problem statement by simply paraphrasing again.

This step called paraphrasing was illustrated in the transcript when the facilitator asked John "Of these four problem statements, would you say back to me the problem statement or combination of problem statements that you would like to get some ideas for solving?"

To practice the technique of highlighting do some Mess-Finding and Data-Finding on a particular challenge on which you wish to work. Use separate sheets for these preparatory stages. Then use any divergent Problem-Finding technique you'd like to practice to develop a list of at least twenty different possible problem statements:

1. _____
2. _____
3. _____
4. _____
5. _____
6. _____
7. _____
8. _____
9. _____
10. _____
11. _____
12. _____
13. _____
14. _____
15. _____
16. _____
17. _____
18. _____
19. _____
20. _____

Now, answer the following questions:

1. What numbers are "hits?" _____

   _____

2. Which hits seem to "relate?" _____

   _____

3. For each group of hits which relate (hot spots), develop a new problem statement:

   _____

   _____

   Hot spot restatement: _____

   _____

   Hot spot restatement: _____

   _____

   Hot spot restatement: _____

   _____

   Hot spot restatement: _____

   _____

4. Choose one restatement for which you'd like to get some ideas or see if you can paraphrase these again to develop *one* common translation for all the hot spots.

   Which hot spot did you choose? _____

   _____

   Were you able to paraphrase all your hot spot restatements into one common translation?

   If so, what was it? _____

   _____

CPF-2: RESTATEMENT

Sometimes you identify only one or two hits after generating a long list of possible statements. In these cases you can move along a little faster by restating a few hits into one comprehensive Idea-Finding statement.

Generate a list of ten possible problem statements for a situation for which you have already done some Mess-Finding and Data-Finding.

1. _____

2. _____

3. _____

4. _____

5. _____

6. _____

7. _____

8. _____

9. _____

10. _____

Identify the two or three most significant "hits" or problem statements for which you want to gather some ideas. Combine the key elements from each statement into a new statement providing a similar perspective on the mess.

Restatement: _____

CPF-3: CHECK FOR IDEA-FINDING POTENTIAL

Occasionally, one problem statement seems to stand out as the best way to view the situation. Frequently it is helpful to evaluate the statement briefly to see if it satisfies the following criteria:

1. Will it lead to lots of ideas?
2. Is it the question about which you want to find ideas?
3. Does it locate the ownership clearly?
4. Is it affirmative in its orientation?
5. Is it free of criteria?
6. Is it stated briefly and clearly?

If the statement appears to fulfill the criteria, you can focus your Idea-Finding efforts productively using that perspective. If the statement seems to fall short on any criteria, perhaps you can modify the statement to strengthen its usefulness for gathering ideas.

PROBLEM-FINDING RESOURCES & REFERENCES

Dillon, J. T. "Problem Finding and Solving." *Journal of Creative Behavior,* 1982, *16 (2),* 97-111.

Einstein, A. and Infeld, L. *The evolution of physics,* NYC: Simon and Schuster, 1938.

Getzels, J. W. "Problem Finding and the Inventiveness of Solutions." *Journal of Creative Behavior,* 1975, *9 (1),* 12-18.

Getzels, J. W. and Csikszentmihalyi, M. *The Creative Vision: A longitudinal study of problem finding in art,* NYC: Wiley, 1976.

Noller, R. B.; Parnes, S. J. and Biondi, A. M. *Creative Actionbook,* NY: Scribners, 1976. (Unit II, pp. 11-16).

Parnes, S. J.; Noller, R. B. and Biondi, A. M. *Guide to Creative Action,* NY: Scribners, 1977. (pp. 47-51 Unit II; pp. 319-324).

Wertheimer, M. *Productive Thinking,* NYC: Harper & Row, 1959.

CHAPTER

Idea-Finding

> **Idea-Finding Stage**
>
> Many alternatives and possibilities for responding to the problem statement are developed and listed. Ideas that seem most promising or interesting are selected.

After studying this chapter, you will be able to:

1. Define and give examples of fluency, flexibility and originality and explain their use in CPS.
2. Identify and explain several important considerations of environment and materials for creative thinking.
3. Define and identify six necessary conditions for productive brainstorming.
4. Describe and apply several specific methods and techniques for generating many ideas, formulating different or varied ideas, developing unusual ideas, or refining and enhancing ideas.
5. Apply specific methods and techniques for idea generation to problem statements of your own.
6. Describe methods and techniques for analyzing the strengths and limitations of ideas and for identifying promising ideas for more detailed evaluation.
7. Apply methods and techniques for recognizing promising ideas to lists of ideas for your own problems.

Idea Finding

Before we move ahead, let's review briefly where we've been so far. In the previous sections, you have studied and practiced specific "tools" (useful methods and techniques) for

- Becoming sensitive to opportunities and challenges on which you want to take some action (Mess-Finding);

- Searching for data and questions to help you better to understand your goals and priorities (Data Finding);

- Formulating specific questions (statements of problems or sub-problems) about which you might want to seek new and potentially useful ideas (Problem-Finding).

Now you should begin gathering some of those ideas – or should you?

Maybe you've selected a problem statement that has really "grabbed" your attention. You're really enthusiastic about it, and some ideas are already starting to pop into your mind. You hurry to write them down before you lose them. When you feel this excited about "Idea-Finding," you'll discover the enjoyment and stimulation often associated with creative thinking; it's really *fun* when lots of ideas are jumping up at you from every direction.

Sometimes you'll get so involved in generating ideas–by yourself or with a group–that you'll be surprised later, when you look back at your long lists of ideas and discover *how much* creative thinking you've done.

But it doesn't always happen that way. Sometimes developing new ideas is sheer drudgery or torture!

What happens? What hinders our efforts to produce ideas? In *Chapter Three*, many different kinds of "blocks" or obstacles to creative thinking were presented. We need to be alert and on guard so these obstacles don't restrict our Idea-Finding.

One of the most common obstacles in Idea-Finding is being "Habit-bound" in our thinking. To some extent, we all have some parts of our everyday behavior that are simply habit-bound; sometimes those habits are helpful and time-saving. For example, there are some things that we just *do* everyday. We really wouldn't want to have to stop every time to think, step-by-step, exactly how to do them. These are things like putting on shoes, brushing teeth, or combing hair. These are habits or "friendly little routines" to help us get things done quickly and efficiently.

These little habits can be amazingly persistent! They can become so routine that we discover we've gotten into a "rut." When you deliberately try to do something differently, it will feel very odd or uncomfortable.

Figure VI-1.

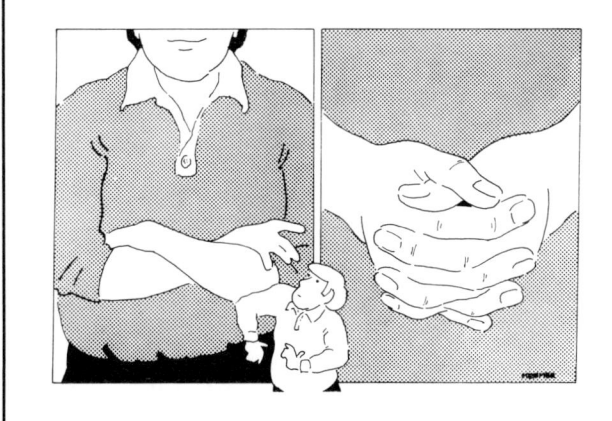

Try these simple exercises, just to see for yourself how persistent some little habits can become:

First, cross your arms in front of you. Which arm is "on top?" Now, unfold your arms, and reverse them, so when they're crossed, the *other* arm is on top. Does it feel comfortable? Most people report that it feels uncomfortable or awkward; some even have considerable difficulty crossing their arms "the wrong way."

Next, fold your hands, as if in prayer. Which thumb is on top? Separate your hands, and re-fold them so the other thumb is on top. How does it feel? Again, many people report that it feels unusual, uncomfortable, or "wrong."

Creative Problem Solving: The Basic Course

Our *thinking* can become just as habit-bound and, as with other habits, that can be both good and bad. When you're trying to think creatively and solve problems, you should want to find fresh, new ideas. In those circumstances, habit-bound thinking can get in the way.

Can you easily identify at least twenty-five kinds of dogs? Answer this question for yourself *before* you look at the list on the next page.

If you were "habit-bound" in your thinking, 25 probably sounded like an awfully large number! You probably thought, "Oh! Goodness, no; I can't identify *that* many dogs!" Then, when you looked at the list on the next page, you probably thought, "Why, of course! I knew 25 of *those* dogs!"

BREAKING AWAY FROM HABIT-BOUND THINKING

How can we break away from habit-bound thinking? Let's start with a simple example. Most likely, you've been to a zoo and noticed that some people throw "snacks" at the animals—often right in front of signs that say, "PLEASE DO NOT FEED THE ANIMALS." Some of these people may not care about the signs, or about the animals either! But many people just don't pay any attention. They've seen the sign so much that they just don't "see" it at all. It's too familiar. Try to break that habit.

PLEASE DO NOT _____ THE ANIMALS
What else might the sign say, besides "FEED"?
List some of your ideas:

_____   _____   _____

_____   _____   _____

_____   _____   _____

_____   _____   _____

_____   _____   _____

Now really S-T-R-E-T-C-H for more ideas; what else could the sign say?

_____   _____   _____

_____   _____   _____

_____   _____   _____

_____   _____   _____

_____   _____   _____

_____   _____   _____

_____   _____   _____

Here's a sample of what one sign says (the imaginative product of someone's creativity at the San Diego Zoo):

⸻

Please Do Not
Annoy,
Torment, Pester, Plague,
Molest, Worry,
Badger, Harry, Harass,
Heckle, Persecute,
Irk,
Bullyrag, Vex, Disquiet,
Grate, Beset,
Bother, Tease, Nettle,
Tantalize;

or

Ruffle
The Animals

⸻

COMMON DOGS

Collie	Beagle	Boxer	Dalmatian
Poodle	Doberman	Greyhound	Bassett
Pomeranian	Spitz	Pointer	Corgi
Black Laborador	Irish Setter	German Shepard	Chihuahua
Dachshund	Weimeraner	Chow	Malamute
Husky	St. Bernard	Great Dane	Cocker Spaniel
Bulldog	Lhasa Apso	Newfoundland	Pekinese
English Sheepdog	Springer Spaniel	Maltese Terrier	Cairn Terrier
Bull Mastif	Scotch Terrier	Manchester Terrier	Golden Laborador

Could you think of several possibilities? Were some unusual? If so, you were breaking away from habit-bound thinking.

> PRINCIPLE: One important rule in creative thinking is—deliberately break away from habit-bound thinking. Ask, "What *else* might be?"

GETTING IN THE RIGHT MOOD FOR IDEA-FINDING

By now, you've learned some useful methods to choose a Mess, to analyze relevant Data, and to formulate specific Problem Statements. After you've selected a certain problem statement on which to work, you're ready for Idea-Finding. As in each stage, however, it's important to insure that the environmental conditions are right and that personally you're ready to start producing ideas. Some specific things will be helpful for you to check or do to begin this stage.

Logistics

When you are planning to use CPS, by yourself or with a group, there are some practical concerns to keep in mind. Do you have everything you need to get started? Do you have the "tools" with which you feel comfortable, including something to help you keep track of your ideas, plenty of flipchart paper and markers?

Firestien and Treffinger (1983, pp. 3-4) offered some suggestions about the "logistics" of an effective CPS session—the props and materials to help insure that things run smoothly and that the environment stimulates thinking. These suggestions included:

- Use plenty of flipchart paper or newsprint, for a handy record of your ideas.

- If you don't have an easel, use masking tape to attach the paper to a wall or chalkboard. (Use several columns of paper, so you can easily move across the wall while writing, and use layers of paper several sheets thick so pauses to put up more paper will be brief.)

- Large crayons are excellent; they're less expensive than markers, and they don't "bleed" through the paper.

- If you're working in a group, arrange yourselves into a "horseshoe" shape, so everyone can easily see the easel or the wall with the paper on it.

- Put a label at the top of each sheet as you begin writing on it (e.g., Problem-Finding #1, or just "PF-1") so after the session, it will be easier to remember the sequence of ideas and events.

- Number each idea as you go along, so it will be easier to "locate" specific ideas for converging.

- As you move from stage to stage, keep the previous sheets in sight, so you can always look back over prior ideas and data.

- Record all ideas as accurately as possible; don't try to "edit" or "correct" suggestions as you write them on the flipcharts.

- If possible, use a "back up" person as a recorder, so your production doesn't get bogged down waiting for the ideas to be written down.

- Everyone in a group should have paper and pencil to keep track of their own ideas, so ideas won't be lost.

- Don't depend on a tape recorded version of the session. The tape can become very difficult to understand and transcribe if several members of a group are letting ideas flow rapidly.

Time

You don't have to do everything in one session, of course, but you should insure that you have enough time to get involved in thinking productively on at least some CPS stages. Also, you may want to take deliberate steps to insure that you won't be interrupted during your session.

Warm-Up

Dr. E. P. Torrance of the University of Georgia has long stressed the importance of taking time to "warm up" or prepare for creative thinking. Creative thinking and problem solving can't be turned on or off like a water tap! An easy way to get yourself ready for creative thinking is to select a simple "practice problem" for divergent thinking before starting work on a real problem. Look out your window, around the room, or at an interesting picture. Ask yourself, "What's happening? What do I see? What *else* might be?" Push yourself to think of several possibilities. Deliberately *practice* "opening up" to search for many ideas. For groups, warm up or "group building" activities and exercises have been provided by Torrance & Myers (1970) and Treffinger, Isaksen, & Firestien (1982). Eberle's (1982) book, *Chip In,* also illustrates an imaginative way to use paint chips (color samples from a paint store) as a creative warm up activity.

Working Alone or in a Group?

Sometimes, you'll be on your own in searching for ideas and solving a problem. Most of the methods and techniques in this Chapter can easily be applied by an individual working alone. Often, however, it may be useful to get some "input" from others, even for a problem that is entirely your own. Others' ideas can help you stretch your thinking, to clear away some habits or other obstacles that block new ideas, to bring new resources to bear on the problem, or just to provide some encouragement and support for your efforts. There are also times when a group's effort can be stimulated by providing time for individuals to break away to do some individual thinking which can later be brought back to the group.

Remember the Ground Rules

In this stage, you'll use the same Ground Rules for divergent and convergent thinking that were discussed in *Chapter Two*. (This would be a good time to review pages 17-20 in *Chapter Two* to refresh your memory. The ground rules are helpful to remember because they'll help you to break away from rigid, habit-bound thinking, and they'll also get you started in the direction of generating really good new ideas, whether you're working alone or in a group.

READY? GET SET. GO!

When you have broken away from barriers or blocks to creative thinking, you may find that Idea-Finding starts quite naturally: ideas just start "flowing freely," and all you have to do is start writing. But even with experienced groups (which we call "process aware" because they are knowledgeable and "tuned in" to the CPS stages), help is sometimes needed to start the idea flow.

To begin, the skillful Idea-Finder uses one or more very specific, useful "tools" to stimulate creative thinking. These tools can be useful in helping us get *more* ideas, which we refer to as *Fluency* in thinking. Or, they can be useful by helping us be less rigid, so we can see the problem from different viewpoints; thinking of different kinds of ideas is described as *Flexibility*. Third, many techniques help us to think of unique, unusual, or "different" ideas—novel possibilities that don't usually occur to us. This kind of thinking is called, *Originality*. Finally, some techniques help expand ideas, adding extra details or refining ideas to make them richer, more complete, more appealing. This is *Elaboration* in thinking.

Asking Open-Ended Questions

One of the first things to practice in thinking divergently is using open-ended questions. They do not have one specific "right or wrong" answer. Instead, they invite us to think of many possibilities. Learning to use these questions helps us become more "fluent" in our thinking–better able to generate a number of possibilities, not just one answer. Often, these questions ask us to speculate about very unexpected or unusual circumstances.

Some examples of open-ended questons are:

1. Name as many round, edible objects as you can.
2. What if it were against the law to laugh?
3. What are some things you could do with old junk automobiles?

There are *many* answers that might be given for each question, and none of the questions has any single "correct" answer.

One of the most popular names for a technique for gathering many ideas is "Brainstorming." Almost anyone who has ever heard or read *anything* about creative thinking has heard about brainstorming. As a matter of fact, some people are a little confused about brainstorming. Some folks seem to think that brainstorming and creative problem solving are the same thing. In reality brainstorming is just one part of creative problem solving–a specific "tool" or technique to be used to generate alternatives and possibilities. Other folks use the word brainstorming as a synonym for several other terms: discuss, tell, share, present, or sometimes for arguments or "bull sessions." However, brainstorming has a very specific meaning and use.

You're "brainstorming" when you are following the ground rules for divergent thinking to generate a list of many possible ideas about any Mess or problem (in *any* stage of CPS, not just in Idea-Finding). There must be:

1. an atmosphere of deferred judgment.
2. an emphasis on quantity.
3. openness to all ideas.
4. deliberate efforts to combine and make new connections.
5. extended effort to produce varied and unusual ideas.
6. willingness to let ideas "simmer" or "incubate."

Diverging Activities: How To Get More and Better Ideas, Part I

Let's try to do some creative thinking. Here are several exercises you can use to practice thinking of many ideas, different kinds of ideas, or new and unusual ideas. It is not necessary for you to do all of these activities; read them over and select several that are interesting.

Write down your answers to keep a count of your ideas. You will find that, as you continue to practice, it will become easier to improve your fluency, or to try deliberately to be more flexible (varied), original, or elaborative in your thinking.

Creative Problem Solving: The Basic Course

DIF-1: WHAT IF/JUST SUPPOSE

When you want to begin finding lots of ideas, you may find that it is helpful to use a question that begins, "What if . . . ." or "Just suppose that . . . ." Here are some samples. For each one, have some fun—let the ideas flow freely, and try to create many responses:

What if it were against the law to sing?

What if every car in the world were painted green?

Just suppose that cats barked and dogs meowed. What would happen?

What if it rained every Friday afternoon?

Just suppose there were no punctuation marks. What would result?

Don't be afraid to be playful in your thinking. These kinds of questions invite us to come up with all kinds of ideas and, if you remember the ground rules for divergent thinking, you won't hold back any of your ideas, no matter how funny, strange, or impractical they might seem.

DIF-2: BRAINSTORMING EXERCISE

Let's practice some brainstorming . . . Suppose you've been asked to serve as a special consultant to the housing/construction industry. It seems that home builders all over the country would like to introduce some new features that will increase peoples' enthusiasm for building new homes or remodeling their present homes. They've been considering a number of changes, and have identified a particular area for which they want lots of new ideas–and they want your help.

"We'd really like to design an *ideal bathroom,*" they tell you. What suggestions can you make? List as many ideas as you can for designing the ideal bathroom. Make a list of your own. Then get a group of friends together and try some group brainstorming.

List your ideas here:

DIF-3: THE ABSENT-MINDED SPOUSE

Two months ago, you forgot about your spouse's birthday. You really got yourself in trouble that time!

It has been a particularly busy week, with lots of unexpected little problems and crises at work, and you've been feeling all day that there was something you were supposed to do, but you couldn't remember what it was. You decided it must just be the general pressure from your busy week.

Now, driving home from the office, as you pull into the driveway, you remember: today is your wedding anniversary. What are you going to do? List several possibilities for dealing with this situation.

Creative Problem Solving: The Basic Course

DIF-4: THE CONCERT

Let's try one more general brainstorming exercise, to help you to really feel confident in your ability to generate *LOTS* of possibilities. This time, try to generate *even more ideas* than you did in any previous exercises. In addition to being as *fluent* as possible, try to get some *original* or unusual ideas, and remember to be *flexible*–look at the problem in a new way, or from a different perspective.

Situation:

You've just heard that your favorite musical group or performer will be giving a concert performance in your town in two weeks. That's really exciting news, because you've never seen them in concert. You're determined to attend the concert. However, when you called the ticket office, the clerk told you, "Oh, those tickets went on sale last Sunday, and they were all gone by noon Monday. They were all snapped up right away."

Last night, there was one classified ad in the newspaper offering a pair of tickets for sale, but the person said he was taking offers and would sell them to the highest bidder at the end of the week. The present high bid was $250.00 for the pair, for which the face value is only $30.00. You can't afford to join the bidding at that price!

Directions:

Before you start Idea-Finding, review the Data and write out some problem statements. After developing a problem statement that seems promising, do some Idea-Finding. Think of as many ideas as possible for this situation. (Enlist some friends to join you for some group brainstorming, if you wish.)

Make a list of your ideas on separate sheets of paper.

Diverging Activities: How To Get More And Better Ideas
Part II - Revving Up The Engine

Brainstorming can be very enjoyable when ideas are flowing fast and furious. But there are times when that doesn't happen—when the production of ideas slows up or grinds to a halt. Fortunately, a skillful Idea-Finder will have access to a number of additional tools for thinking that will promote effectiveness in generating new, varied, and unique possibilities.

You won't need to use every tool each time you work on a problem, of course. Instead, as you gain experience with the process, you'll learn to select tools that seem to be particularly promising for the challenge on which you're working.

If the problem calls for *lots* of ideas, and you're having trouble thinking of many, you'll want to stress *finding more possibilities*. You will want to use a technique that will help you increase the sheer *quantity* of ideas you produce. Exercise DIF-6 will help you practice the SCAMPER technique, which can be especially useful for generating many ideas.

When all your ideas seem to be alike or to fit in the same category, you probably need to change the pace by emphasizing flexibility. You will want techniques that help you change your viewpoint, look at things in a new way, or approach the problem differently. Exercise DIF-5 provides an opportunity for you to use ATTRIBUTE LISTING, which can be very helpful for looking at problems from various perspectives.

If many of your ideas seem to be ordinary and obvious, and you want some new possibilities that are much newer, fresher, or more unique, you will be searching for techniques that emphasize originality. You want to use techniques that really encourage you to stretch your imagination and be more adventurous in your thinking. Exercise DIF-7 presents the FORCED RELATIONSHIPS strategy, which can be especially helpful for developing unusual or highly original possibilities.

Creative Problem Solving: The Basic Course

DIF-5: ATTRIBUTE LISTING – SLIDE PROJECTOR

Most of us are familiar with a 35mm slide projector. They're used in schools, businesses, and for slide shows in many homes. Let's assign ourselves the task of improving that familiar piece of audiovisual equipment. (If you get a fortune for selling your ideas for this exercise to a large photographic equipment manufacturer, please remember the authors!)

In What Ways Might We Improve the slide projector?

Begin by doing some brainstorming, just to warm up for the task:

_____   _____

_____   _____

_____   _____

_____   _____

Now, try to get some *different* ideas by using Attribute Listing. To do this, consider first the major parts of components (or "attributes") of any slide projector. Make a general list, and don't worry about how "correct" it is; different people might define the attributes differently. For example, we might say the attributes of a slide projector are:

Slide contianer (box or tray)	Focusing mechanism
Projection lens	Fan
Projection system (mirrors, etc.)	Power source (motor, cord, switch, etc.)
Cabinet and legs or "feet"	Slide "advance" mechanism (manual/remote/automatic)

Take each of these attributes, one at a time, and try to find several new and different ideas that might occur to you for improving the slide projector.

ATTRIBUTE   **IDEA(S) FOR IMPROVEMENT**

Slide container (box or tray)

Projection Lens

Projection system

Cabinet/Legs

Focusing Mechanism

Fan

Power Source

Slide Advance Mechanism

104

DIF-6: SCAMPER: AN IDEA CHECKLIST

When you need to stimulate fluency, and to develop plenty of new ideas, using an "Idea Checklist" can be helpful. You can use almost any list of words or questions to help trigger some directions or ideas that you hadn't considered before.

Alex F. Osborn (1953) developed a list of "Idea Spurring Questions" for this purpose, and the key words from that list were cleverly arranged and used by Bob Eberle (1971) to help us generate many ideas. Eberle used the word "SCAMPER" as a mnemonic device (to help us remember the words by having each letter of SCAMPER stand for an Idea-Spurring word).

Here are the words that Eberle used for SCAMPER:

S	=	Substitute?
C	=	Combine?
A	=	Adapt?
M	=	Modify? Magnify? Minify?
P	=	Put to other uses?
E	=	Eliminate?
R	=	Reverse? Rearrange?

You could use other words for each letter, of course, as long as the words help stimulate your thinking. Can you find some other words for each letter of SCAMPER that might be useful to you in getting new ideas? Write them in the list and use them!

When you are starting to run out of ideas for a problem, try using each of the SCAMPER words, one at a time. Try to make some new connections in your mind. What ideas are triggered by the word? For example, when you think of "Substitute," ask, "What might I do instead? What else might I use? What could be replaced or done differently?" Then, let your mind stretch for some new possibilities for your problem. Do the same thing for all the SCAMPER words. If one doesn't suggest any new ideas, go on to the next. Go back and forth freely among the words; it's not necessary to use them in order.

Let's take a problem for which we might want to get some ideas, and then try out the SCAMPER technique for using an Idea Checklist.

In What Ways Might We improve toothpicks?

Write down the first ideas coming to mind:

_____

_____

_____

_____

_____

Now, try SCAMPERing. Read each of the SCAMPER words and try to think of *more* improvements for toothpicks that might be suggested.

SUBSTITUTE . . . . _____

_____

_____

_____

_____

COMBINE .... _____

ADAPT .... _____

MODIFY/MAGNIFY/MINIFY .... _____

PUT TO OTHER USES .... _____

ELIMINATE .... _____

REVERSE OR REARRANGE .... _____

Creative Problem Solving: The Basic Course

DIF-7: FORCED RELATIONSHIPS

Sometimes it's difficult to think of different or unusual ideas. To increase your originality, try some methods and techniques that really help "stretch" your thinking and take you down paths you hadn't noticed before. One way to do that is by using "Forced Relationships" methods.

That doesn't mean that you're going to be held at gun-point to get ideas; it merely suggests that you're forcing yourself to find new "connections" by considering possibilities that might not occur spontaneously—"forcing" the problem together with an object or element that wouldn't usually be joined to it. Give it a try.

Situation: Three neighborhood cats of unknown ownership have been serenading you every night at three in the morning. You're sick of it . . . and getting tired, too! What can you do about it?

Brainstorm for some possibilities:

_____

_____

_____

_____

Next, consider each of several objects that (we're sure you'll agree) aren't usually associated at all with this situation. For each, try to make some new, interesting and unusual connections. What does each object suggest to you that might have anything at all to do with the problem? What brand new and original ideas can you develop?

A Candle _____

_____

_____

_____

An ancient manual typewriter _____

_____

_____

_____

A box of peanut brittle _____

_____

_____

_____

Creative Problem Solving: The Basic Course

Owner's manual for an Edsel   _____

                                     _____

                                     _____

                                     _____

An el deluxe cigar   _____

                                     _____

                                     _____

                                     _____

A sailboat   _____

                                     _____

                                     _____

                                     _____

The first time you consider each of these items, you may think of some obvious puns or play-on-words responses. That's fine! Write them down and play with them. How might they relate to the situation? What new ideas can you create?

After you've been through the list once, go back to the beginning and think again about each object. Stretch for new connections.

To vary the technique, consider other sources of objects you could use for "forced relationships." Some possibilities include the dictionary, advertising sections of newspapers, old magazines, or mail order catalogues. Take the first few objects that catch your eye; *don't* try to select objects that seem to "fit" the problem.

Diverging Activities: How To Get More And Better Ideas
Part III - Now It's Time For "Super Stretch"

Sometimes, even with all these tools at your disposal, you may find that you still aren't generating pleasing and productive ideas. Perhaps there still are too few ideas, or maybe they're all variations on the same theme, or none of the ideas are really novel or interesting. In these situations, be ready to do some SUPER STRETCHING in your thinking!

Creative Problem Solving: The Basic Course

DIF-8: MORPHOLOGICAL ANALYSIS: THE WRITER'S FRIEND

People who write "continuing" or serial material (columnists, writers for television soap operas or sitcoms, etc.) have often reported that it is difficult to produce a steady flow of new material. Their dilemma can be useful in illustrating a good method for generating *lots* of ideas for a problem, including many unusual possibilities, using a very simple procedure: morphological analysis. No, that's not the study of morphs. It relates to morphology–studying form or structure.

It can be used with any problem in which there are several major parts or components (called "parameters" of the problem) for which a variety of attributes might exist. That's almost *any* problem!

Let's write a story as an example.

Begin by assuming there will be four major parameters in your story: characters, places, goals, and obstacles. Use the chart to fill in the attributes for each parameter.

	MORPHOLOGICAL MATRIX			
	Character	**Places**	**Goals**	**Obstacles**
1				
2				
3				
4				
5				
6				
7				
8				
9				
10				

Start with *Characters*. In the first column, list ten characters (any ten! any kind of characters!) for a story. (Examples to get you started: Fido the dog, an ugly bartender, a pirate . . . .)

Next, block out the first column so the ideas won't get in your way. Then, in Column Two, list ten different *places* where a story might take place. ANY ten places; don't worry about anything you wrote in the first column.

Third, after blocking out the first two columns, fill in Column Three by listing ten *Goals* that might be major concerns in a story. Once again, list ANY kinds of goals—let your ideas flow freely, and don't be limited by anything in the other columns.

Fourth, after covering the first three columns, think about some *Obstacles*. Think about anything that might be an obstacle or a source of difficulty or concern to someone in a story. Who might be some people who are obstacles? (Villains . . . which ones? Enemies? Relatives?) What might be some other personal, emotional, or situational obstacles? (health? personality characteristics? disasters?) List ten obstacles in Column Four.

It's time to get your story. Write down your phone number:

_ _ _ - _ _ _ - _ _ _ _

These are the numbers that
"count" - the last four digits!

Using the last four digits of your phone, pick:

    a character   (the first digit, using the corresponding number from Column One)

    a place   (the second digit, matched with Column Two)

    a goal   (third digit, matched with Column Three)

    and an obstacle   (last digit, matched with Column Four).

Think about your four choices. Put them together. Get an image for a story in your mind. Now, write *your* story:

_____

_____

_____

_____

_____

_____

_____

_____

_____

_____

_____

_____

How many possible stories were there in the morphological chart? There are 10x10x10x10 or 10,000 possible combinations! Within that large number of combinations, there's enough material to take you through quite a few typewriter ribbons. When we're trying to "Super Stretch" for ideas, this technique generates many unusual combinations. Some will be much more productive or valuable than others, of course. Even if only 10% of the possibilities were to prove useful, that would still yield 1,000 ideas! Compare that to a sample list of only 10 ideas, from which only 2 or 3 might be useful, and you can easily recognize the potential value of the technique.

Converging Activities: Converging Tools for Idea-Finding

Sometimes the only thing worse than not having enough ideas is feeling that you have "too many!" Of course, you probably can't really have too many good ideas, but the problem is often, "How can I sort through all these pages of possibilities and locate those that seem most promising for closer evaluation or for future development?" To do this, it's important to remember the ground rules for convergent thinking (in *Chapter Two*). Some *convergent* tools can also be helpful.

CIF-1: FINDING THE 'HITS'

The first way to approach your list of ideas is easy and not very technical: simply take a crayon or marker, look over your list of ideas, and put a mark (such as a checkmark or a star, or circle ideas) to identify all the ideas that just seem to jump out at you as being appealing, promising, or worthy of more detailed consideration. These are the "Hits;" they're ideas that are obviously interesting and attractive to you. This isn't a very rigorous, scientific-approach, but it can be surprising how effective a little bit of personal good judgment can be. Don't sell yourself short!

Take any of the lists of ideas you generated for any of the diverging exercises in this chapter. Look through it, selecting ideas that are "Hits," and marking them. You will most likely spot several promising ideas easily.

CIF-2: A-L-U

There are times when you will want to examine your list of ideas more closely, even before you begin Solution-Finding (in which all your promising ideas will undergo much more extensive analysis, evaluation, and development). You may have so many that you need to sort them out and take stock of your progress, or perhaps you really aren't certain how to tell which ones might hold the greatest potential. In these situations, A-L-U can be a helpful technique. A-L-U stands for: Advantages, Limitations, and Unique connections.

ADVANTAGES – Ask (for your list, or for any specific ideas you're reviewing) what *advantages* does this idea offer? What are its strongest points? What makes it attractive or appealing? What potential do I see in it?

_____

_____

_____

_____

LIMITATIONS – Next ask, what *limitations* are there? Are there obvious flaws or weaknesses to be overcome if we work with this idea? Are there possible trouble spots? What might limit the attractiveness or effectiveness of this alternative?

_____

_____

_____

_____

UNIQUE CONNECTIONS – Finally, ask yourself, "Does this idea suggest any new or unusual connections I wasn't aware of before?" Are there any "hidden potentials" here?

_____

_____

_____

_____

These questions can help you select promising ideas for further consideration and development.

CIF-3: HOT SPOTS, RELATES, AND PARAPHRASE[1]

You will also find that any of the converging techniques introduced in *Chapters Four and Five* (as well as those that follow in *Chapters Seven and Eight*) can also be used in Idea-Finding.

Take a Mess on which you worked in Data-Finding and/or Problem-Finding, and use a specific problem statement to generate a list of Ideas. Put some of the Idea-Finding diverging techniques to work! Then, review the converging techniques from other *chapters* and use them again to analyze your list from Idea-Finding.

Do NOT look for one idea that is the "best one." This isn't a popularity contest or an idea-slaughtering! The major goal of converging in Idea-Finding is to help you to develop a manageable number of promising ideas to take to the next steps of the process.

List your ideas: _____

---

[1] We acknowledge the contributions of Multiple Resource Associates for the development of these techniques; see Treffinger, Isaksen, and Firestein (1982) for additional details.

REFERENCES CITED

Eberle, B. *SCAMPER.* Buffalo, NY: DOK, 1971.
Eberle, B. *Chip In.* Carthage, IL: *Good Apple,* 1982.
Osborn, A. F. *Applied Imagination.* New York: Scribners, 1953.
Torrance, E. P. & Myers, R. F. *Creative Learning and Teaching.* New York: Dodd-Mead, 1970.
Treffinger, D. J., Isaksen, S. G., & Firestien, R. L. (eds.). *Handbook of Creative Learning.* Honeoye, NY: Center for Creative Learning, 1982.

CHAPTER 7

Solution-Finding

> **Solution-Finding Stage**
>
> Many possible criteria are formulated for reviewing and evaluating ideas. Several important criteria are selected and used to evaluate, strengthen and refine ideas.

After studying this chapter, you will be able to:

1. Explain the purpose of the Solution-Finding stage in CPS.
2. Define criteria and their use in Solution-Finding.
3. Identify sources and categories of criteria for Solution-Finding.
4. Generate a variety of criteria.
5. Select the most important criteria for your problem.
6. Apply a grid or matrix for using criteria to evaluate ideas systematically.
7. Explain and give examples of the three different uses of criteria (screening, selecting and supporting ideas).
8. Distinguish criteria that are essential for evaluating ideas from those that are primarily useful for polishing ideas.
9. Explain and use several alternative Solution-Finding methods.
10. Identify strengths and weaknesses of possible solutions in preparation for Acceptance-Finding.
11. Apply criteria to analyze and evaluate several possible solutions for a problem of your own.

Solution-Finding

During Idea-Finding (*Chapter Six*) you generated many options or possibilities in response to a Problem-Finding question. Using methods and techniques from *Chapter Four* and the ground rules in *Chapter Two,* you can generate an extensive collection of promising ideas for any problem statement. But, within this "pool" of ideas, there will undoubtedly be a great deal of variety. Some ideas may be unique or novel, others more obvious. Some may be more valuable than others. But which ones are really the most promising? If you generated many options during Idea-Finding, you will now be able to compare and analyze those possibilities and select a manageable set of alternatives to develop and use.

The goal of the Solution-Finding stage of CPS is to help you do that analysis and develop alternatives in a smooth and systematic way. Your aim is not to "kill" ideas, but to look closely and critically at the ideas upon which you converged during Idea-Finding. Thus, you use the Solution-Finding stage of CPS to:

- compare many alternatives;
- compare *desires* (wants) with *demands* (needs);
- examine the "pros" and "cons" of several ideas;
- narrow the options to a manageable group;
- determine the strengths and weaknesses of ideas, to help "build" or develop their best features;
- screen ideas for possible modifications or improvements;
- reject options you do not wish to consider further;
- select or decide upon your most promising possibilities (MPP).

We hope you've noticed that we have deliberately avoided suggesting that Solution-Finding is just getting "THE ONE BEST IDEA." Good Solution-Finding is not just negative, rigidly judgmental, but is selective in choosing options. You are forming a good solution by evaluating, modifying, comparing, assessing, building and improving. Of course, you will be rejecting some options while *choosing* to work with others. You're trying to create a more favorable ratio of strengths to weaknesses, and to give ideas the best possible head start towards successful implementation planning. This stance is consistent with "affirmative judgment" in the convergent ground rules in *Chapter Two*.

This affirmative posture can be illustrated through the following example. Suppose you were to end your Idea-Finding efforts with ten "hits." If the emphasis of your thinking was primarily negative or critical, you could probably find good reasons to eliminate all ten ideas. If you search hard enough for a reason *not* to do something, you will generally end up by doing nothing! This is *not* the purpose for engaging in Solution-Finding. A more affirmative attitude encourages you to search for aspects of several (or all!) of the ten ideas which had some potential to satisfy or solve the problem. These positive elements could be combined and built into tentative solutions. The strengths and weaknesses of these potential solutions can then be examined. To build on ideas' strengths and to overcome their weaknesses is what this stage is all about!

In this stage, you're using your *creative* thinking skills to diverge and consider many possible criteria for examining your ideas. You're also using *critical* thinking abilities. It may be necessary, however, to make a shift in your understanding of "critical thinking." Too often, people associate critical thinking only with very detailed, precise, inflexible, judgmental thinking. They tend to *equate* critical thinking with *criticism*. Of course, the critical thinker must be rigorous, precise, and logical. But these skills can be used affirmatively and constructively as well as in an arbitrary, destructive kind of criticism. Throughout Solution-Finding, as well as in the converging phase of all the CPS stages, you should remember "Affirmative Judgment" and the other ground rules for converging (see *Chapter Two*).

USE OF CRITERIA

A criterion is a standard, rule, test or means upon which a judgment or decision can be based. These measures or yardsticks help you decide to use, modify or reject certain ideas. Criteria come from many sources including accumulated knowledge, values and attitudes, perceptions, feelings and observations. They may be explicit, as when you are buying a new car; or implicit, as when you select a particular pair of shoes to wear or a piece of candy from a box. Some criteria might be very important to consider in one situation and perhaps almost insignificant in another.

During CPS you will find it helpful to generate *many* criteria. These may come from examining some of your selected ideas, either from Idea-Finding or from your overall perceptions of the situation. The important task is simply to generate a good, complete list of all the criteria which might help you develop a promising solution for the problem.

During Solution-Finding, criteria are used to *screen, select,* and *support* options for which you will eventually be developing a Plan of Action. If you have already made some choices during the convergent phase of Idea-Finding, chances are you may have used criteria in reaching your decision. Sometimes the use of certain criteria remain hidden during decision-making. For example, briefly check to see what kind of shoes you are wearing right now. You've probably made a choice about this (assuming you own more than one or two pairs of shoes). Take a moment to write down *why* you selected today's footwear.

Reason 1 _____

Reason 2 _____

Reason 3 _____

Your reasons might include the following:

1. It is snowing or raining.
2. This pair is more comfortable than my others.
3. They will keep my feet dry and warm.
4. They match the colors I am wearing.
5. They look nice.

Each reason has a potential criterion within it. For example, the five sample reasons can be converted into criteria:

REASON	CRITERION (Will it . . .)
1. It is snowing or raining.	1. be consistent with weather?
2. This pair is more comfortable than my others.	2. be personally comfortable?
3. They will keep my feet dry and warm.	3. be personally comfortable?
4. They match the colors I am wearing.	4. match my outfit?
5. They look nice.	5. be appealing?

Notice that criteria are really means by which you can assess or measure the appropriateness or usefulness of various options. They are also key elements in a question of the form, "WILL IT . . . " (or in this case, "WILL THEY . . . "). For example, in our footwear decision, the first criterion would fit the question: "WILL THEY BE CONSISTENT WITH WHAT THE WEATHER DEMANDS?" For purposes of listing criteria, we recommend that this be "headlined" or shortened into a few key words, like "be consistent with weather." Try converting your reasons for choosing what you are wearing into criteria:

Criteria 1 (from Reason 1) _____

Criteria 2 (from Reason 2) _____

Criteria 3 (from Reason 3) _____

In this simple, everyday situation, you most likely used criteria to *screen* your available options. This process helps you to sift through the possibilities and provides the "raw material" for scrutinizing your options. Thus, *screening ideas or options* constitutes the first use of criteria. Within this use, criteria provide the basis of comparison for making your decision.

Screening means observing your options using your criteria as lenses. For example, if you were to look over the shoes, boots, slippers or sneakers in your closet, you would be screening your options. Before that screening effort, you might even have forgotten about some of your options. ("Oh, gee . . . *that* pair! I forgot I had them!") An additional benefit can be that screening helps bring many options to your attention. You will then use your criteria to screen those, to identify the options you wish to consider further.

Once you have screened available options, a second use of criteria comes into play: *selecting from among alternatives*. This use focuses on separating out the options which appear to meet the criteria from those that don't. In our example, after you screened or scanned your closet, you could sort your options into a number of categories. A general sorting might involve deciding which options have potential and which do not. For example, if it were snowing and "consistent with weather" were a criterion, you might select a few pairs of boots or old shoes, but you would by-pass the sandals. Once the selections have been made from promising possibilities, you are ready for the third use of criteria.

The third use of criteria is *supporting your selected options*. Supporting means finding ways to strengthen, sharpen, simplify, solidify, streamline, shape, or substantiate options. Your focus will be on studying the selected ideas and evaluating their strengths and weaknesses. This also provides the means to modify alternatives, if necessary, to satisfy your criteria more effectively.

Perhaps you considered a particular pair of boots for a cold, snowy day. But, as you considered them, you realized they weren't very high and thus, might not provide you with the necessary warmth. If "Will they keep me warm and comfortable?" had been a criterion, you could support your option by finding ways to increase warmth and comfort, despite the fact that the boots were short. For example, you might decide to wear some high, warm thermal socks.

TYPES OF CRITERIA

There are many different types of criteria. Depending on the challenge you are considering, the nature of the most significant data regarding the situation, your definition of the problem, the quality and quantity of alternatives available, and the consequences or importance of your decision, the criteria you will consider may vary. Therefore, we can share with you some very general, common categories of criteria, although your actual choices will usually be unique.

1. *COST* – "Will it cost too much?" This includes a variety of specific questions. Again, the specific form of the criteria will vary considerably from one circumstance to another. For example, if your budget is fixed and no other resources appear to be available, you may list the specific dollar amount: "Will the cost exceed $xxx.xx?" Another way to deal with the cost criterion is to determine the cost of each option and then examine how the options meet the other criteria. In this way you could determine the relative advantage of the options in comparison with their cost. Alternatively, there may be some situations where all you can do is estimate costs and simply assign a subjective value to your options. For example, you could use the rankings of "advantageous," "acceptable," or "unacceptable" to place a relative value on the cost of your selected options. The aim of this category is to help you get some indication of the strengths or weaknesses of each option in relation to cost, financial outlay, or perhaps even savings. In other words, using the "cost" criterion helps you consider more productively the old issue, "How much is *too* much?"

2. *TIME* – "Will it take too much time?" Again, how much is too much? Again, the specific form of these criteria will vary greatly over many situations. It can be useful to specify what is meant by "time" when evaluating ideas using criteria in this group. For example, you may really be most concerned that your option must be put into place within a specific time, perhaps two or three days. In this case, your specific time criterion may be "Will it be possible to accomplish this option within three days?" Some of your options might seem more easily accomplished within that time frame, but you may still wish to examine some of the others to determine if they could be modified to be accomplished within that time frame. The purpose of criteria in the time category is to get a general picture of the time-

quality balance for each option. The more time you take to do a job, the more effort you can devote to the quality of the job. However, because time is *always* limited, you must make a personal judgment about the appropriateness of the alternatives you choose to use, or the jobs to be done.

3. *FEASIBILITY* – "Will it work?" Can the idea be accomplished? This criterion deals with the realm of possibility. Is it believable that the alternative will actually do what is intended?

4. *ACCEPTABILITY* – "Will I like it?" "Will others like it?" The general criterion of acceptability deals with your level of willingness to take an idea and use it. This type of criteria focuses on your own willingness to accept a particular option as well as your perception of how it might be accepted by others.

5. *USEFULNESS* – "Will it be beneficial?" This type focuses on the general level of value that various options might have to fit some purpose, make some gain, or create some benefit.

While specific form of each criterion varies from one problem to another, the following basic guidelines may be useful for generating criteria:

1. **BE RELEVANT.** Use your knowledge and awareness of the situation to shape your criteria.

2. **BE CLEAR.** Be sure to state your criteria so they are easily understood.

3. **BE CONCISE.** Be certain to express the most essential aspect of each criterion.

4. **BE CONSISTENT.** Once you apply a certain meaning to a criterion be sure to continue using it the same way throughout the evaluation process.

Diverging Activities

The divergent phase of Solution-Finding includes generating many different criteria which *might* be used to evaluate your ideas. Apply the ground rules for diverging described in *Chapter Two;* they will assist you in coming up with a variety of criteria.

It is important to diverge during this stage to prepare yourself to screen, select and support your choices. Your most promising ideas will eventually be formed into a detailed Plan of Action. If you have really stretched your thinking during Idea-Finding you have undoubtedly come up with a *wide* variety of alternatives. It is especially important for you to generate many criteria to provide a basis for reviewing thoroughly all the options. Careful attention to Solution-Finding assists you in being more explicit in your decision-making and enables you to take the fullest advantage of the potential of *all* your ideas.

DSF-1: BRAINSTORMING CRITERIA

One way to develop many different criteria is to use the technique of brainstorming completions to the question: "Will the idea_____?" For example, let's say you were interested in finding better ways to show affection to someone you care for. Take some time to generate at least 25 different ideas for the question: "In What Ways Might I Show Affection?"

1. _____
2. _____
3. _____
4. _____
5. _____
6. _____
7. _____
8. _____
9. _____
10. _____
11. _____
12. _____
13. _____
14. _____
15. _____
16. _____
17. _____
18. _____
19. _____
20. _____
21. _____
22. _____
23. _____

24. _____

25. _____

When you have finished generating your ideas, develop at least 20 possible criteria for evaluating your idea. Remember to BRAINSTORM . . . everything goes, NO criticism, strive for quantity (20), free wheel, and combine!

Criteria for evaluating the ways to show affection . . . "Will the idea . . . ."

1. _____   11. _____
2. _____   12. _____
3. _____   13. _____
4. _____   14. _____
5. _____   15. _____
6. _____   16. _____
7. _____   17. _____
8. _____   18. _____
9. _____   19. _____
10. _____   20. _____

DSF-2: USING CRITERIA CHECKLISTS

It is nearly impossible to develop a checklist to include criteria necessary to examine all the ideas for any problem situation. But when time is of the essence or if you just want a place to get started, checklists can be very helpful.

The following checklist provides you with 50 questions spread over the five types of criteria mentioned earlier. Use this list to see if you have generated enough of your own criteria. Many broad categories are sometimes used in discussions of idea evaluation. These include descriptors like practical, interesting, attractive, etc. The following lists suggest several general categories but also include specific questions to use in formulating criteria. *Feel free to add, subtract, or modify any criteria on the list to better meet your specific requirements.*

COST –
Will the idea . . .
1. cost more than our budget allows?
2. reduce costs in the future?
3. cause me to liquidate certain investments prematurely?
4. entail marketing costs?
5. involve many personnel?
6. cost enough to promote the idea of value?
7. provide ways to share costs?
8. have costs that are tax-deductible?
9. have costs that can be planned for over time?
10. provide enough benefit to outweigh the cost?

TIME –
Will the idea . . .
1. be possible to put into operation shortly?
2. allow me to meet my deadline?
3. be timely?
4. be better if done later?
5. be better if done sooner?
6. last or endure?
7. take too long to explain?
8. take too much time in order to achieve quality?
9. be a permanent or long-lasting one?
10. involve a long-term commitment of resources?

FEASIBILITY –
Will the idea . . .
1. be operationally sound?
2. take more facilities or resources than I have?
3. work in actual practice?
4. do the job?
5. be possible to make happen?
6. be functional?
7. be manageable?
8. get out of control?
9. be suitable?
10. be capable of being dealt with successfully?

ACCEPTABILITY –
Will the idea . . .
1. be simple, direct and unsophisticated?
2. be compatible with human nature?
3. be acceptable without lengthy explanation?
4. provide some variations in its use?
5. be consistent with accepted values and attitudes?
6. "explode" in peoples' minds?
7. allow the leadership to go along with it?
8. allow others to endorse it?
9. be a "right" idea or product for the organization?
10. create circumstances that may be difficult to accept?

USEFULNESS –
Will the idea . . .
1. meet a real need?
2. provide some long or short-range benefits?
3. provide some new or original way and at the same time fit into what is currently being done?
4. be profitable?
5. improve methods of operation, conditions, or safety?
6. prevent or eliminate waste or conserve the use of materials?
7. increase production or sales?
8. improve the quality of output?
9. be more efficient to use?
10. prove more advantageous than others?

OTHER CATEGORIES –
Will the idea . . .
1. _____
2. _____
3. _____
4. _____
5. _____
6. _____
7. _____
8. _____
9. _____
10. _____

Converging Activities

There are actually two convergent phases in Solution-Finding. First, you choose the criteria that seem most important to consider for evaluating your ideas. This is "convergence on criteria (CC)." Second, you use those criteria to evaluate systematically the options generated during Idea-Finding. This is "convergence for analysis (CA)." Convergence during the Solution-Finding stage of CPS provides a foundation for effective evaluation of alternatives, and also provides the starting point for strengthening and refining your most attractive or promising ideas. This concern for *idea-development* helps you to prepare for successful implementation planning during the next stage (Acceptance-Finding).

CC-SF-1: WEIGHTING CRITERIA

As you can readily observe after generating a wide variety of criteria, not all are of equal importance. Some may be so important that you may wish to use them to form two major groups: acceptable ideas and unacceptable ideas. Other criteria may vary in importance but provide some measure for ranking ideas. One way to provide an indication of the relative importance of criteria is to use the Paired Comparison Analysis (PCA) technique.

1. First, go back to exercise DSF-1 on page 6 in this *Chapter*. Remember that you generated 20 different criteria to be used to evaluate your options for showing affection to someone. From the 20 you generated, select nine which you feel have potential to evaluate your alternatives.
2. Take these nine criteria and place them on the left side of the PCA grid on this page. One criterion would be next to the letter "A" another next to the letter "B" and so on.
3. Now, follow the directions under the PCA grid.

PAIRED COMPARISON ANALYSIS

CRITERIA

[PCA triangular grid with rows/columns labeled A through I, and Sum of Scores column on the right for A through I]

1 - SLIGHTLY more important
2 - MODERATELY more important
3 - MUCH more important

Consider only the two criteria represented by each box formed by the intersection of the two axes of the grid. (*Example:* the left-most box on the top row is A&B, the box farthest to the right is A&I, the left-most box in the third row is C&D.)

1. Compare the two criteria represented by each box and decide which is more important in your judgment.
2. Place the letter corresponding to the more important criteria in the box.

3. Using the scale at the left of the grid assign a weight (or degree of importance) to the letter . . . you are now saying how much more important one criterion is over another.
4. Complete the grid by considering each box (pair of criteria) progressing from left to right and top to bottom.
5. Total the numerical scores received by each criterion (letter) to obtain the raw weights of the factors (proportional weights may be derived by using the lowest score as one and calculating the rest). Use the horizontal and vertical rows labeled by the letter under consideration.

(Adapted from Treffinger, Isaksen & Firestien, 1982, p. 121.)

When you finish, you will have a numerical rating of the relative importance of the nine criteria under consideration. Although the numbers give the appearance of an objective approach, keep in mind that these numbers merely represent your personal or subjective judgment, not an absolute, authoritative ranking.

One of the authors used this approach in an attempt to "objectify" the criteria to be used in evaluating homes for purchase. A house was found to meet *all* the criteria and some money was even invested in making estimates of various improvements and repairs needed. However, after three visits to the house, another and even more important criterion was discovered. The house didn't seem to "grab" the author's wife. Despite the fact that the option scored well on all the so-called "objective criteria," it was not an appropriate choice.

Rather than take the rankings as coming from some objective or external source, keep in mind that *you* have to exercise control over them! Use of the PCA technique provides some important information regarding your criteria. For example, depending upon which criteria score at the highest level, you may wish to make these your "sorting" criteria. The others may be used for the ranking function. But remember, you make the decisions regarding their interpretation and application.

CC-SF-2: SORTING CRITERIA

Another way to select and sort the criteria you developed during the divergent phase of Solution-Finding is to determine which are "MUSTS" and which are "WANTS." This sorting process will also provide information about the relative importance of your criteria.

The criteria you judge to be "MUSTS" are the most important to consider. They may come from certain situational constraints over which you have no control. They can also come from considerations over which you exercise a great deal of control and which you consider to be of utmost value in analyzing your alternatives. These criteria may be so important that they will lead you to evaluate your options on a "go/no go" basis. They *must* be satisfied by *any* possible solution before it can be considered seriously for implementation.

"WANTS" are criteria you would *like* to consider. These are criteria you would like to use to "test" ideas, to see how some ideas measure up against your standards, hopes, or expectations. These are the "added factors" that may provide good information about turning an adequate or ordinary idea into an exciting plan. These criteria, which we'll call "WANTS," help you define how to *modify* ideas so they will perform better on those criteria. These are the criteria you want to use to "polish" or refine ideas, once the "MUST" criteria have been satisfied. (You could try to modify some ideas that don't satisfy the "MUST" criteria, but experience suggests that your efforts may be better placed elsewhere!)

Select one of the three scenarios below (A, B or C) and try to generate at least 20 possible criteria.

A. List your ideas for the Problem-Finding question: "In What Ways Might I organize my time?" Then proceed to Part I of the exercise.
B. List your criteria for what makes the "perfect vacation" and place them in Part I of the exercise.
C. YOUR CHOICE – Generate 20 different criteria in Part I of the exercise using a problem or situation of your choice.

PART I - Generate a list of criteria on _____

1. _____   11. _____
2. _____   12. _____
3. _____   13. _____
4. _____   14. _____
5. _____   15. _____
6. _____   16. _____
7. _____   17. _____
8. _____   18. _____
9. _____   19. _____
10. _____   20. _____

Creative Problem Solving: The Basic Course

PART II: Separate selected criteria into MUSTS and WANTS

MUSTS   Standards or conditions the options *have* to meet or satisfy.

WANTS   Standards it would be nice if they met

1. _____

2. _____

3. _____

4. _____

5. _____

1. _____

2. _____

3. _____

4. _____

5. _____

The second convergent phase of Solution-Finding uses the selected criteria to examine and analyze ideas. Many people are good "intuitors" in that they can implicitly and internally consider all the criteria and examine their options "from the gut-level" and develop their most favored option or most promising possibilities (MPP). Not everyone is so fortunate, however, and some find out (often unhappily!) that they aren't as good as they thought they were when their plan doesn't work out very well! We recommend that you become familiar with several systematic methods for evaluating your ideas. These "Convergent Analysis" activities will help you, and you can use the tools whenever you find it appropriate.

CA-SF-1: USING A GRID

Once you have selected your most important criteria, you are ready to use a systematic and explicit approach to analyzing the worth and value of your Idea-Finding alternatives. A Solution-Finding Matrix can be useful. The rows of the matrix can be used, for example, for your ideas, and the columns can be used for your criteria. Examine the following sample grid:

CRITERIA

IDEAS	A	B	C
#1			
#2			
#3			

The grid provides the *structure* for your efforts at analyzing and evaluating the ideas. There are a variety of ways to use this structure. One of the first choices you need to make is what scale you are going to use. Keep it simple, especially at first! A few of your options are:

1. A, B, C, D, F
2. +, −, √
3. ☺ 😐 ☹
4. 1 - 10 (1 = low; 10 = perfection)
5. Excellent, Very Good, Satisfactory, Needs Improvement
6. 1 - 5 (1 = low; 5 = excellent)

For our sample Solution-Finding Matrix, we have chosen to use a scale of 1 - 5 so that:

1 = unacceptable
2 = needs improvement
3 = satisfactory
4 = very good
5 = excellent

The most productive approach in using the matrix is to begin with the first criterion, and use it to examine all the ideas. Then, proceed to the next criterion, and so on, until the matrix is full. This may help you to avoid the natural tendency to rate ideas quickly as high or low on *every* criterion just because their first rating or two were high or low. By rating all ideas against *one criterion at a time,* you are actually making comparisons among ideas. This helps produce more realistic ratings. See the example below:

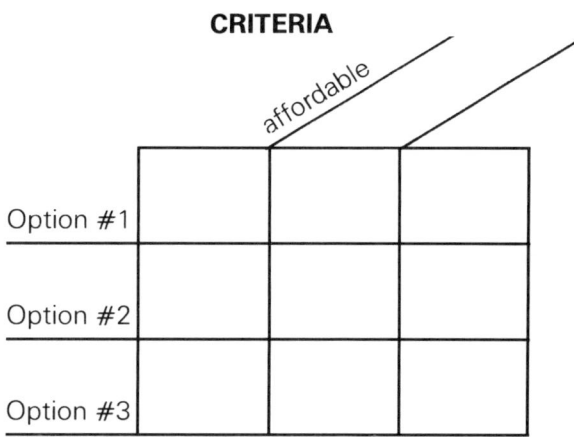

To see how we completed the sample matrix below, let's consider a sample:

MESS:
    Getting from the airport into New York City for a one-day business meeting.

HIGHLIGHTED DATA:
- I'm a self-employed sole-proprietor.
- I have just arrived at LaGuardia Airport for a one-day seminar at a midtown hotel.
- Taxi fare will be about $20 one way.
- The airport bus to a central city location is $7.50.
- A rental car costs $42.95 per day with unlimited mileage.
- The airport is too far from my destination to permit walking.
- At the airport I've met three acquaintances going to the same conference.
- Parking in the city is expensive and scarce.
- The airport bus runs every 20 minutes with a return schedule unknown.

SELECTED PROBLEM STATEMENT:
    In What Ways Might I make the airport-conference round trip?

SUMMARY OF SELECTED IDEAS:
-   Take a taxi alone.
- * Share a taxi.
- * Share a car rental.
-   Rent my own car.
- * Take the airport bus.

Using the selected ideas (marked with an asterisk), we've constructed the following Solution-Finding matrix:

CRITERIA

IDEAS	affordable	quick	convenient
Share Taxi	5 ($10 per person for round trip for 4)	5 (right there)	4 (need to meet at fixed time)
Share Car Rental	3 ($13.50 each with parking)	2 (paper work to get car)	2 (parking, getting car and meeting)
Take Bus	2 ($15 round trip)	3 (at airport, but have to wait)	3 (need to find out where and when to get bus)

After considering the results of using the matrix, it seems that sharing the taxi with your acquaintances is the best option - and that might be quite correct.

However, don't let a total score dictate a decision for you. There may be some circumstances, for example, that should lead you to consider other possibilities. Some examples include:

1. You may not like the acquaintances—they may all be smoking cigars!
2. They may have other plans.
3. They're planning to leave the conference early for cocktails.

Or, on a real problem, your options may be more diverse and there may be several promising alternatives coming close in final score. The "scores" the ideas were assigned will provide you the basis for comparing the strengths and weaknesses of your options. It may be fruitful to use this information to modify or improve your options to build them up.

```
                         time          cost
        IDEA #1      5    4    4    1    4

        IDEA #2      1    4    4    5    4
```

In this example, the two options may have the same final score, but each clearly has different strengths and weaknesses. The focus of your efforts ought to be how to improve the cost of Idea #1 or how to accomplish Idea #2 within a shorter time frame.

Using a matrix to analyze your options may provide a brand new idea. It is appropriate to generate this new idea during Solution-Finding, especially if it responds better to the criteria under consideration. Some groups using CPS for the first time say "We're in Solution-Finding–you can't come up with any more ideas now!" This kind of thinking clearly violates the "spirit" and purpose of the Solution-Finding stage!

Another possibility in using the matrix is that the ideas under consideration may be combined using the particular strengths and weaknesses discovered during the evaluation process. In the example above, Idea #1 may have something to offer Idea #2 in terms of the time criterion and vice versa for cost. Feel free to combine entire ideas or even certain key elements of ideas during Solution-Finding.

Now take a few sheets of paper. Mark each one for one of the stages, and try your *own* "run-through" from Mess-Finding all the way through to Idea-Finding. Create a good list of ideas, and then select ten or so that you would like to consider further. Generate a list of criteria using one of the techniques presented in this chapter. Finally, select several criteria (try for 6-8!) to apply by using a Solution-Finding Matrix. (See the next page for a sample matrix.)

Remember: 1. Work column-by-column, so you compare *all* ideas on a single criterion at a time.
2. Avoid the "sum trap" and use your scoring system to examine the *strengths* and *weaknesses* of your options.
3. Use the "Decision" portion of the matrix to mark ideas you wish to consider using right away (check the "use now" area); ideas you think may be modified or combined with others (check the "modify-hold" area); or ideas you choose to reject.

Converging in this manner during Solution-Finding provides the raw material with which to develop an effective Plan of Action during the next stage of CPS (Acceptance-Finding).

The matrix is not the only converging tool for Solution-Finding. Any converging tools from the other CPS stages can be applied to this stage. Any of these converging tools (like Paired Comparison Analysis, finding advantages, limitations and unique connections; or others) used within the general guidelines for converging found in *Chapter Two* can be effective. They may require slight modification, but all try to help you choose, select, judge or evaluate options.

Creative Problem Solving: The Basic Course

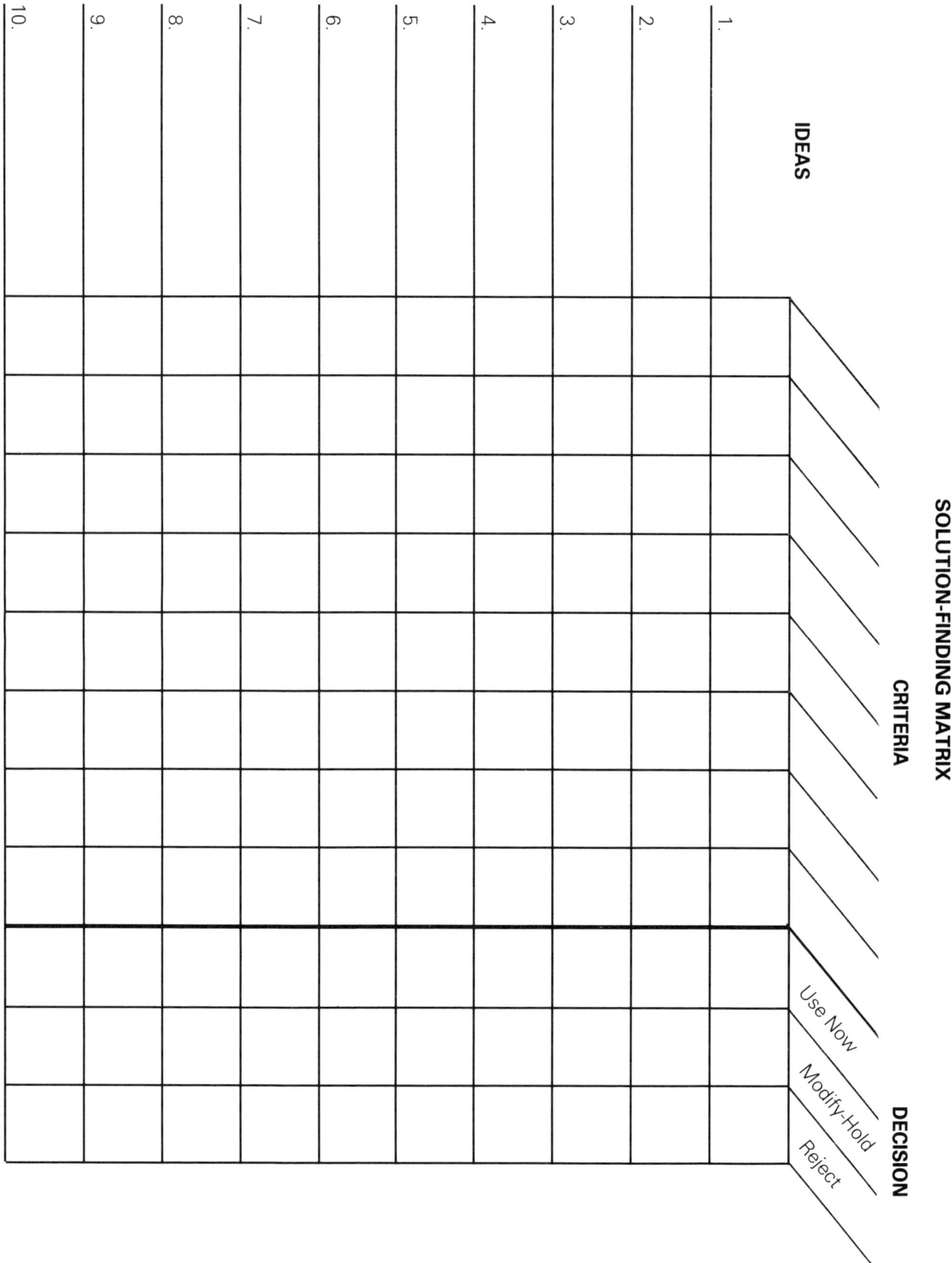

CHAPTER 8

Acceptance-Finding

> **Acceptance-Finding Stage**
>
> Possible sources of assistance and resistance are considered and potential implementation steps are identified. Most promising solutions are focused and prepared for action by formulating specific plans for action.

After studying this chapter, you will be able to:

1. Define the purposes and importance of Acceptance-Finding.
2. Identify and consider many possible sources of assistance and resistance for potential solutions to problems.
3. Develop a list of several possible actions or responses which might be considered for each source of assistance and resistance.
4. Formulate a general plan for implementing solutions.
5. Identify potential obstacles or difficulties which might influence implementation of your plan.
6. Identify ways to prevent obstacles from arising and to overcome them if they do occur.
7. Formulate revised Plans of Action with specific steps to be taken, including:
    A. a 24-hour step;
    B. short-term actions;
    C. long-term actions.

Acceptance-Finding

WHAT IS ACCEPTANCE-FINDING?

When you've finished Solution-Finding, you have selected the most promising or appealing possibilities for solving a problem. However, you're not quite ready to "leave the process" and use that solution. Solution-Finding helped you to screen alternatives, select from your options, and strengthen or develop your ideas. Now you should consider Acceptance-Finding, the final stage of CPS. Its focus is to generate ways to promote successful *implementation* of your most promising solution. The result of your Acceptance-Finding efforts will be a Plan of Action. Your Plan of Action will help to insure that the solution will be acceptable to you and others, and that you have a careful, thoughtful, and practical plan containing specific steps to be taken.

Acceptance-Finding helps you examine your tentative solution, to build upon its positive aspects, overcome its limitations, and eventually take effective action.

Acceptance-Finding includes:

- putting your plan into action;
- achieving your solution(s);
- putting it all together so you can actually *do* it;
- planning to achieve the actual final product;
- after action is taken, comparing actions with planned outcomes;
- detecting potential and actual flaws in your plan and making appropriate improvements;
- reviewing actions to determine where or how to proceed;
- knowing how to determine if your plan is successful.

WHY IS ACCEPTANCE-FINDING IMPORTANT?

Throughout your problem-solving efforts, much of your energy and effort has involved understanding the situation (Mess-Finding), gathering and ordering important information (Data-Finding), defining the problem (Problem-Finding), generating alternatives (Idea-Finding), and evaluating potential solutions (Solution-Finding). Most of the effort has been focused on the situation and your own perceptions of the data, problems, and ideas. Solution-Finding provided evaluative information on your own personal acceptance of the solution. Acceptance-Finding is important because it helps you make the solution acceptable to others as well.

Another reason Acceptance-Finding is important is that it prepares ideas for use. Having a solution is really only a starting point. During Acceptance-Finding you have an opportunity to develop a *plan* to assist in actual implementation of ideas. Such a plan can be helpful in communicating with others and gaining their acceptance.

Spending time to build a Plan of Action allows you to take time to consider many factors leading to success. If you just take a solution and run, without Acceptance-Finding, you risk overlooking many important concerns. By examining your Plan of Action, anticipating potential concerns, and preparing methods of overcoming them, you can increase the likelihood of successful acceptance. In effect, you are actually spending a little time now, to avoid spending more time solving future problems. Acceptance-Finding helps insure that you have considered many details that promote successful problem solving.

Diverging Activities

As in each of the other CPS steps, Acceptance-Finding begins with a diverging phase. This is a deliberate effort to identify many people, places, objects, times, reasons, and actions that might aid or hinder implementation of your plan. You should stretch to consider many ideas, not just a few that come most easily to mind.

DAF-1: ASSISTERS AND RESISTERS

Begin by identifying your most promising solution (from the Solution-Finding stage). For that solution, use the "Planning for Acceptance" matrix on the next page to identify elements of *assistance* and *resistance*. Elements of assistance are:

WHO — People (individuals, groups, organizations, etc.) who might help.
WHAT — Things, objects, or activities that might be helpful to use in implementing your solution.
WHERE — Locations, places, or events which might be preferred/or especially useful for your situation.
WHEN — Times or aspects of timing (dates, deadlines, schedules, etc.) which might be beneficial or especially appropriate.
WHY — Reasons you can provide for implementing your solution; especially reasons you think will promote support for your solution.
HOW — Steps or specific actions which need to be accomplished in order to carry out your solution effectively.

Elements of resistance are:

WHO — People (individuals, groups, or organizations) who might oppose, inhibit, or limit the effectiveness of your plan.
WHAT — Things, objects, or activities that might impede your progress.
WHERE — Locations or places which might not be appropriate or helpful in implementing your solution.
WHEN — Particular times to avoid, or aspects of timing which might cause concerns when implementing your decision.
WHY — Reasons for implementing your solution that might not meet wide agreement; reasons for not accepting the solution.
HOW — Actions or activities that might operate against your solutions or that promote failure.

Assistance and resistance can be listed by generating ideas through brainstorming or other diverging strategies. The important thing is that you *stretch* your thinking to obtain many elements for your consideration. These elements provide a survey of the resources and concerns at your disposal for developing a Plan of Action.

Now, try this planning technique by starting with a solution to a problem. Use the "Planning for Acceptance" matrix on the next page.

After you have listed many sources of assistance and resistance, you should identify those of greatest importance. You may find some overlap among the items in your matrix. For example, the most important person to provide you assistance might also be the most important person to provide resistance. These overlapping elements are *keys* to building an effective Plan of Action; you must consider your actions very carefully in these areas.

Once you have identified the most important elements for your planning, develop a Plan of Action which would include:

A. At least one *immediate* action you can take to get started with implementation (a *24-hour action step*).
B. Some short-term actions (the steps to take *soon*).
C. Some long-term actions; including some ideas about "How you will know if your plan is working well?"

PLANNING FOR ACCEPTANCE

PROMISING IDEAS/ACTIONS:

	SOURCES OF ASSISTANCE	SOURCES OF RESISTANCE
WHO (People)		
WHAT (Things)		
WHERE (Places)		
WHEN (Times)		
WHY (Reasons)		
HOW (Actions)		

PLAN OF ACTION: A. _____   C. _____
 B. _____   _____
 _____   _____
 _____

Creative Problem Solving: The Basic Course

DAF-2: PLANNING FOR ACCEPTANCE

You can also list assisters and resisters to help you generate possible actions when your promising solution involves several ideas or subparts.

1. After converging phase of Solution-Finding for any problem, you might have several ideas which could be implemented singly, sequentially, or in combination.
2. For each component, list several possible sources of assistance and resistance (using the same procedure as in Exercise DAF-1).
3. Next, for each block in the chart, develop a list of possible steps you might consider. These might be steps to assure agreement and support, sell the ideas to others, or overcome obstacles and concerns. List these under "Specific Steps to Consider" in each block.

PLANNING FOR ACTION MATRIX

COMPONENTS OF PROMISING SOLUTION

Idea #_____	ASSISTANCE	RESISTANCE
	SPECIFIC STEPS TO CONSIDER 1. _____ 2. _____ 3. _____	

Idea #_____	ASSISTANCE	RESISTANCE
	SPECIFIC STEPS TO CONSIDER 1. _____ 2. _____ 3. _____	

Idea #_____	ASSISTANCE	RESISTANCE
	SPECIFIC STEPS TO CONSIDER 1. _____ 2. _____ 3. _____	

DAF-3: USING CRITERIA TO BUILD SUCCESS

Some people seem to think that the criteria in Solution-Finding are used only to evaluate ideas, and that it isn't necessary to look at them again after you've finished Solution-Finding.

Quite to the contrary, your Solution-Finding criteria can be very helpful to you in Acceptance-Finding. Here's how:

1. Begin by reviewing the converging phase of Solution-Finding from any of the exercises in Chapter Seven or for a problem of your own.
2. Examine the idea (or ideas) that were selected when you determined your most promising solution.
   a. On which Solution-Finding criteria were your promising ideas *strongest* or *best*?
      These criteria might help you identify *strengths* on which you can build in Acceptance-Finding. List some strengths or positive features suggested by the criteria:

      _____
      _____
      _____
      _____
      _____
      _____
      _____

   b. On which Solution-Finding criteria were your promising ideas *weakest* or *poorest*?
      These criteria might help you identify *concerns* which you should seek to overcome. List some of the *limitations* or *concerns* suggested by these criteria:

      _____
      _____
      _____
      _____
      _____
      _____
      _____

Creative Problem Solving: The Basic Course

DAF-4: PLANNING FOR SUCCESS*

Having a well-developed written Plan of Action may be all you need for certain problems. It may also be important, however, to identify the areas in which your Plan might be especially vulnerable. What might go wrong? What are some of the difficulties that might arise? What's the worst imaginable thing that could happen?

1. Ask, "What might happen if_____?"

2. Generate five to ten questions in this form regarding your Plan of Action.

_____
_____
_____
_____
_____

These questions point toward specific areas of concern you haven't previously considered.

3. Next ask, "Which of those concerns might be most likely to occur?" Rate each question, using this scale:

    VL = Very Likely to Occur
    ML = Moderately Likely
    MU = Moderately Unlikely
    VU = Very Unlikely

4. Ask, "How critical would it be if this *did* happen?" Rate each question using this scale:

    D = Disaster!
    T = Troublesome
    N = Nuisance
    I = Inconsequential

5. Consider each of your questions from Part 2, as you have rated them in Parts 3 and 4.

    How likely are they to occur?
    How serious would they be?

Decide for yourself which *three* represent your greatest concerns. These will be areas that you believe should receive additional attention in planning to assure success.

Your three primary areas of concern are:

_____
_____
_____

---

*The idea for this activity is adapted from "Potential Problem Analysis" techniques described in: Kepner, C. H. & Tregoe, B. B., *The New Rational Manager*. Princeton, NJ: Princeton Research Press, 1981.

6. For the three areas you selected in Part 5, complete this chart:

AREA OF CONCERN	HOW TO PREVENT IT...	HOW TO RESPOND IF IT HAPPENS...
1.	a.	a.
	b.	b.
	c.	c.
	d.	d.
	e.	e.
2.	a.	a.
	b.	b.
	c.	c.
	d.	d.
	e.	e.
3.	a.	a.
	b.	b.
	c.	c.
	d.	d.
	e.	e.

If the preventative actions succeed, your concerns will have been overcome. If they don't succeed, you will be able to use the actions generated in the "How To Respond If It Happens..." column.

Creative Problem Solving: The Basic Course

DAF-5: IMAGING FOR SUCCESS*

Effective implementation or Action Planning can be stimulated by the use of imagery. You may find this technique particularly helpful in planning to gain acceptance by others.

Imaging for Success has five steps:

1. *GOAL DISCOVERY.* Think about the goals you would like to attain through your Plan of Action. List them in your mind.

2. *ENCOUNTER DISCOVERY.* Consider the people who will be involved in gaining acceptance of your solution. Picture them in your mind. Where are they? Where and when do you usually see them? What do they look like? How do they sound? What are their particular habits, likes, dislikes?

3. *APPROACH AND REACTION DISCOVERY.* Imagine that you're meeting with each of these individuals. Picture in your mind the setting, your appearance and action, and the other person's. What are you doing and saying? What reaction do you perceive? Try to vary your approach, and feel the effects. To help you imagine, try to "reverse your role" (i.e., react as you believe you would in the other person's role).

4. *REFINEMENT DISCOVERY.* Consider the effects or impact of the approaches that you tried. How did various individuals react? What responses were positive? Negative? How might you modify, refine, or improve your approach?

5. *PLANNING AND REHEARSAL DISCOVERY.* For the revised actions you consider most promising, what details should you remember? (Consider time, place, mood, materials, preferences, etc.) Rehearse in your mind an entire scenario for successful execution of your plans.

---

*Adapted from: Lesio, P. J. "Imaging for Success." Unpublished Masters Project, State University College at Buffalo, New York, August, 1984.

CONVERGENCE IN ACCEPTANCE-FINDING

Convergence in Acceptance-Finding is important because it focuses and directs the action that should occur to implement your solution(s). For this reason, it is essential to evaluate your Plan carefully before putting it into action.

Many people are interested in how new ideas are communicated and accepted by others. In fact, with an increase in interest in the innovation process in organizations and individuals, has come increased concern for studying communication to promote acceptance of new ideas; this area of study is called "diffusion of innovations."

When the book *Diffusion of Innovations* was published in 1962, there were 405 publications about this topic available in the literature (Rogers, 1983). By the end of 1983, there were more than 3,000 publications about diffusion, many of which were scientific investigations of the diffusion process.

Rogers (1983) described diffusion as an information exchange occurring as a convergence process involving interpersonal networks. He asserted that the diffusion of innovation is a social process for communicating information about new ideas.

Why is Diffusion Important?

Diffusion is the type of communication which is concerned with innovations (ideas, practices, or objects that are perceived as being new). Acceptance-Finding is the stage of CPS which deals with putting innovations (new ideas and solutions) into practice. Thus, information about diffusion of innovations can be used to guide you in developing more effective Plans of Action. Even though all innovations are not the same, Rogers (1983) identified specific attributes of innovations and examined how these effect acceptance. He described these characteristics as: relative advantage, compatibility, complexity, trialability, and observability (Rogers, 1983, pp. 210-240).

Relative Advantage is the measure of how much better an innovation is than the idea or object it replaces. This can be expressed in terms of cost, profitability, improved status, etc. People who will be adopting a new idea want to know how much better it is than previous ideas.

Diffusion scholars have found that relative advantage is one of the best predictors of an innovation's acceptance and use by others. The specific dimensions of relative advantage include degree of profitability, low cost, decrease in discomfort, savings in time and effort, and how soon the reward of use occurs. There is a strong, positive relationship between an innovation's relative advantage and its success rate for adoption.

Compatibility is the consistency of a new idea or object with current values, past experiences, and needs of those who will be potential adopters. Generally, the more compatible the innovation is, the more it is adopted.

Complexity relates to the difficulty of understanding and using an innovation. The more complex a new idea or object, the less likely it will be accepted and used.

Diffusion researchers have found this characteristic to be more strongly related to how ideas are adopted than all the others except relative advantage. The general advice to keep things simple appears to be warranted.

Trialability is a characteristic involving the degree of experimentation that can be conducted with new ideas or objects. Some new ideas are limited in the degree to which experimentation is possible, and others must be an "all or nothing" arrangement. Some innovations are more difficult than others to subdivide, try out, modify, or field test.

Diffusion researchers have found that the easier it is to try out or experiment with an innovation, the better the rate of adoption. This may be the case because an innovation that can be modified or used experimentally offers more flexibility and control for the potential adopter.

Observability is the characteristic of new ideas and objects that deals with the innovation's visibility to others. Some ideas provide results which are easily observed and communicated to others; others may be extremely complex and difficult for others to understand. Rogers suggested that the level of observability of an innovation, as seen by others, is positively related to its diffusion. The more readily an innovation can be observed and understood, the greater the likelihood of its adoption.

Other Variables. Although the first five categories account for many of the reasons why individuals choose to accept innovation, there are also other variables which have an impact on the diffusion of new ideas. The relative speed with which a new idea is adopted by others is referred to as the *rate of adoption*. This is generally measured as the number of people who adopt a new idea in a specified period. Other variables include:

1. The number of people involved in making a decision.
2. The type of communication used:
   a. mass media
   b. word of mouth
   c. etc.
3. The environment or culture.
4. Who is supporting (or selling) the new idea or object.

These variables have not been researched extensively by those interested in diffusion, but they will undoubtedly have an effect on acceptance of solutions.

These categories of criteria for diffusion of innovations can be useful in preparing your Plan of Action. An implementation checklist can assist you in evaluating your Plan of Action; such a checklist is provided in Exercise CAF-1.

Converging Activities:

The following pages contain some converging activities for Acceptance-Finding.

CAF-1: IMPLEMENTATION CHECKLIST

These questions will assist you in examining the effectiveness of your Plan of Action.

Relative Advantage
1. Does the Plan point out why it is better than what is currently being used or done?
2. What advantages or benefits might there be to accepting the Plan?
3. Who may be in the position to gain from the Plan?
4. How will I (or others) be rewarded by adopting the Plan?
5. How might I emphasize the Plan's benefits to all?

Compatibility
1. In what ways is the Plan consistent with current practice or thinking? How can this be demonstrated?
2. How can I show that the Plan meets the needs of a particular group?
3. Is the Plan a better way to reach an already commonly-shared goal?
4. What group(s) would naturally endorse the Plan and agree with its goals and actions?
5. Can the Plan be named or packaged so that it might be more favorably accepted?

Complexity
1. Is the Plan easy to understand by others?
2. Can it be explained clearly to many different people?
3. Does the Plan take a long time to communicate to others?
4. How might the Plan be made simpler, and easier to understand? What points might be clarified?
5. Can I demonstrate the ease of use of the new idea or object?

Trialability
1. Are there means for the adopter to try out a section of the Plan before deciding to use the whole Plan?
2. How might uncertainty be reduced concerning the new elements of the Plan?
3. How might you respond if your Plan requires adoption in full, if the adopters want to try out a small piece?
4. How might you encourage adopters to try out part of your Plan?
5. How might you change or modify your Plan to make it more easily tried?

Observability
1. How easy is it for an adopter to find or obtain the Plan? Is it visible?
2. Can the Plan be made more visible to others? How?
3. How might I make the Plan easier for others to understand?
4. How might I best communicate the Plan of Action?
5. Are there good reasons for not making the Plan visible now?

Other questions to help gain acceptance for your Plan:
1. What other resources could be of assistance? How might I best put them to use?
2. What important obstacles must be considered in implementing the Plan? What could be done to overcome them?
3. Will the Plan create new challenges or opportunities? How might you deal with them?
4. What first steps might be taken to initiate action? What might be some next steps?
5. How might I build some feedback into the Plan so that future action can be taken to correct, improve, or modify the approach?

You could easily add to or modify any of these questions. Read through the entire list. Do any of the items trigger new questions to help you improve the acceptance level of your Plan? If so, consider them in addition to the other questions!

CAF-2: CHECKING FOR OWNERSHIP

Once a Plan of Action has been developed, you should check it carefully to insure that there is sufficient ownership and personal meaning to make it both new and useful. One way to examine your Plan is similar to the strategies you used in the convergent phase of Mess-Finding. You can check your Plan to assure you have adequate *influence, interest,* and *imagination.*

A. State your Plan of Action:

   24-Hour Step _____

   Short-Range Step(s) _____

   _____

   Long-Range Step(s) _____

   _____

B. Check your Plan for elements of ownership:

   1. *INFLUENCE:* Does your Plan establish a situation for which you have responsibility and decision-making authority?

      ☐ Yes   ☐ No   ☐ Don't Know

   *If *yes,* continue to respond to the remaining questions.
   **If *no* or *don't know,* can you modify your Plan so that you do clearly claim some personal "clout" for the situation?

   Note: This is a very important aspect of your Plan. Without some element of influence, it is highly unlikely that you will be in the position to actually implement your Plan.

   2. *INTEREST:* Are you willing and motivated to spend the necessary personal energy to implement your Plan?

      ☐ Yes   ☐ No   ☐ Don't Know

   *If *yes,* continue to respond to the remaining question.
   **If *no* or *don't know,* you need to re-examine your Plan to check that you chose to address the most appropriate elements of assistance and resistance. If you did, then you need to go back to review your Problem-Finding efforts. Did you solve the problem you really wanted to solve?

   3. *IMAGINATION:* Does your Plan provide you a novel perspective, viewpoint, or direction toward your situation?

      ☐ Yes   ☐ No

   *If *yes,* double-check your first starting actions toward implementing your Plan, and then *get started*!
   **If *no,* you may have chosen a definition of your problem which remained generally at the same level as your prior efforts. Perhaps you need to see if there are some other problem statements that take you beyond that pattern. Another possibility is that there wasn't enough "stretch" during the diverging phases of the process. If you think this might be the case, double-check the guidelines for divergence (*Chapter Two*) and some of the super-stretch activities outlined in the Idea-Finding chapter (*Chapter Six*).

CAF-3: PLANNING AND PRIORITIZING FIRST STEPS

Another way to converge during Acceptance-Finding is to start with your best option(s) from Solution-Finding and generate a list of specific actions you need to take to put that idea into action. Then, you have several options:

   A. *CHARTING.* You can write each of these actions out on a 3x5 card and then place them in the most appropriate sequence.

   B. *PAIRED COMPARISON ANALYSIS* (PCA). You could use a PCA grid to evaluate the importance of each of the actions you developed.

   C. *OTHERS.* Any of the converging activities can be modified so that you can carefully examine, evaluate, and prioritize the steps you will take to implement your solution (i.e., the four outlook questions on pages 38 and 39 in *Chapter Three* can be easily modified to examine your Plan rather than your statement of the "Mess").

CAF-4: RECYCLING YOUR PLAN

Perhaps you feel that you're "finished" with CPS when you reach Acceptance-Finding. Remember, however, that CPS is a flexible and useful tool in identifying and meeting challenges. By devoting your energy to the CPS process you have discovered some new areas, and you may find yourself with a Plan which takes you to unfamiliar territory. At this point, CPS can continue to be valuable. Acceptance-Finding does not provide you the "end" of your thinking efforts. No Plan you develop should be thought of as "perfect" or absolutely final. Instead, Acceptance-Finding provides you the opportunity to identify sources of outcomes you'd like to achieve or obstacles you need to overcome.

You might have recognized these words from *Chapter Three* on Mess-Finding. As the words suggest, you may discover that your Plan from one Mess can provide the raw material for more Mess-Finding. Each Plan can become the beginning point for a new application of CPS.

Try this activity to illustrate the cyclical nature of the process:

1. *SEARCH.* Find any article in a newspaper or magazine which purports to share a new plan or idea, ready for implementation.

2. *RESEARCH.* Read the article and list several possible Outcomes and Obstacles suggested by the proposed plan.

3. *RUN THROUGH.* Run through Data-Finding, Problem-Finding, Idea-Finding, Solution-Finding, and Acceptance-Finding using one of those Outcome or Obstacle statements for the new Mess.

Not all Plans will require that you recycle through the entire CPS process. You may identify a few key concerns about your Plan and then generate a number of options to deal with those areas. "Closure" occurs when you're ready to start *acting* on your Plan. The chart on the following page will help you in listing your actions.

Creative Problem Solving: The Basic Course

AREAS OF CONCERN	OPTIONS FOR DEALING WITH THIS CONCERN
A.	1.
	2.
	3.
	4.
	5.
B.	1.
	2.
	3.
	4.
	5.
C.	1.
	2.
	3.
	4.
	5.
D.	1.
	2.
	3.
	4.
	5.

REFERENCES CITED

Rogers, E. M. *Diffusion of Innovations.* New York: The Free Press, 1983.

CHAPTER

Putting it All Together

After studying this chapter, you will be able to:

1. Explain the interrelationships among the stages of the CPS process.
2. Use all six CPS stages together in solving a problem of your own.
3. Use CPS concepts and methods with confidence and efficiency in dealing with problems in which time is limited.
4. Determine the best starting point to use in the CPS process for various challenges and concerns.

Putting it All Together

During your study of the first eight chapters of this book, you worked gradually through all six stages of CPS, emphasizing one stage at a time. By now, you should know some specific methods and techniques you can use for Mess-Finding (*Chapter Three*), Data-Finding (*Chapter Four*), Problem-Finding (*Chapter Five*), Idea-Finding (*Chapter Six*), Solution-Finding (*Chapter Seven*), and Acceptance-Finding (*Chapter Eight*). The specific methods you've studied in each of those chapters should be quite useful as you work on a wide variety of opportunities and challenges. Many of those techniques are "tools" you will be able to use in many different situations, even when you may not want or need to go through the entire process.

You should also remember, however, that this book has presented only a *sampling* of the methods and techniques that can be used in solving problems creatively. We hope you will remain alert for new ways to modify and use the methods and techniques in the book, as well as to add new methods and techniques. CPS can serve as a broad, flexible framework for organizing, synthesizing, and applying many tools from a variety of models.

In this chapter, our major goal is to help you to recognize that all of the separate components or "buckets" of CPS can fit together smoothly and effectively. We don't want you to think of CPS only as isolated techniques or fragmented steps. CPS will be much more powerful for you as an integrated approach—a systematic way of organizing and using your tools for creative and critical thinking to solve problems. We want you to be able to focus on the "whole picture." For example, think of CPS not just as a set of separate "buckets," but as a waterwheel, in which all the smaller containers contribute to the overall effectiveness of the machine. Each separate bucket's water contributes to an overall "flow" that produces greater energy and value as a system.

Your understanding and use of CPS will be more effective and rewarding as you become more confident and proficient in using all six stages as a coordinated, flowing process.

In order to accomplish this synthesis, to enable you to be both skillful and confident in your CPS work, four steps will be taken in this chapter:

1. We'll present summaries of three *examples* of the CPS process in action, from Mess-Finding through Acceptance-Finding;
2. We'll provide an opportunity for you to work through the entire process on a problem of your own, using material in the chapter to guide you through each stage;
3. We'll give you a few practice problems to use to build your skill and efficiency in applying the process to a wide range of challenges and problems, even with the constraints and demands of limited time ("Snap Decision Making");
4. We'll provide guidelines to decide whether a particular Mess calls for you to use the entire CPS process, or, if not, to determine the best place in the process to begin.

After you've completed this chapter, we're confident that you will be able to use CPS skills and methods productively in creative thinking and problem solving. Of course, you still won't know *all* there is to know about CPS. We've been using CPS ourselves for many years, and we learn some new things every time we work on a problem. After each CPS session, we sit down to review the session, and to ask such questions as:

* What went well? What were the best parts of the session?
* Why did I do certain things during the session? What were my reactions (and those of others if it was a group session)?
* What could have been improved or handled more effectively?
* How could the session have been made better or more productive?
* Were there any interesting things in this session that we've never discovered before? What were they? How did they work? How might they best be incorporated into future efforts?

If you want to keep extending your CPS knowledge and skill, you'll find some resources and suggestions for further reading and study listed in *Appendix A*.

EXAMPLES OF CPS IN ACTION

The time required for a full "run through" of the entire CPS process depends on many factors: the skill of the problem solver (or, in a group, the skill of the facilitator and the group members), the magnitude and importance of the problem, the time available, etc. When a group is really "cooking" with the process, thoughts flow rapidly and many ideas are generated and collected during each stage. As you can certainly imagine, that can mean *lots* of writing, and plenty of filled up pages of newsprint or flip-chart paper! A full, rich CPS session is very difficult to "capture" in the limited pages of a book. In this section, we have merely provided a *summary* or "capsule" version of a few samples of CPS so you'll have at least a general overview of how all six stages work together. We have streamlined them as much as possible, to make them concise but still illustrative of the divergent and convergent phases of each stage.

These examples may not appear to provide high level "breakthroughs," such as creative solutions that win Nobel Prizes or save hundreds of thousands of dollars for large businesses. There are many such examples of solutions of major dimensions accomplished using CPS. In this introduction, however, our goal is merely to provide you with illustrations of effective applications of CPS in practical, day-to-day situations. The first example is taken from a CPS session with children and the second is from a group of college students. The third example involves a business-related CPS application. While the first two examples are given in summary form, the third example uses several of the worksheets you can use to work on problems of your own. (These worksheets are presented and discussed in detail later in the chapter.) Although the groups and the problems are quite different from each other in many ways (complexity of the problem, impact, maturity of the problem-solvers, etc.), they also illustrate many commonalties— "threads" that are involved whenever the CPS process is used.

SAMPLE CPS RUN-THROUGH: STUDENTS

MESS-FINDING

Diverge I'd like to find a project to conduct on my own.
I'm interested in all kinds of games, sports, outdoor activities.
I'd like to get involved in something new. I've been looking at a new Kite Store in our Community.

Converge My general area of interest is a project about KITES.

DATA-FINDING

Diverge What do I know, think, feel, wonder about KITES?

1. They fly.
2. They're light but sturdy.
3. They can be fun to fly.
4. Ben Franklin flew kites.
5. Some kids can't get them to fly successfully.
6. Fairly easy to build.
7. Charlie Brown's kite gets tangled in trees.
8. Open fields are best.
9. Need a windy day.
10. Could do learning centers about kites.
11. Lots of kids probably don't know how to make/fly kites.
12. They come in many shapes.
13. China/Japan - unusual kites.
14. Wonder what keeps them up?
15. Kites need a tail.
16. Could use movies or displays.
17. Kites provide fun, excitement.
18. We could start a Kite Club.
19. Can we use kites to make money?
20. What was the highest kite ever flown?

Converge "Famous" Kite Flyers – #4, #7, #13.
Learning Kite Making – #5, #6, #10, #11, #16, #18
I think that learning how to make and fly kites seems most interesting to me.

PROBLEM-FINDING

Diverge In What Ways Might I (IWWMI . . .):

. . . make kites for myself? . . . rent kites to other kids?
. . . start kite-making classes? . . . help little kids make kites?
. . . get my kites to stay up? . . . promote safer kite flying?
. . . demonstrate good kite flying? . . . help kids improve kites?
. . . show everyone how to make kites? . . . get kids excited about kites?
. . . make kites enjoyable for me and for others?

Converge I want to learn *and* share with others, so I'll ask, IN WHAT WAYS MIGHT I help other kids to learn to make and fly kites?

IDEA-FINDING

Diverge
1. Show movies.
2. Make kite flying movie.
3. Make a slide show.
4. Make Video program.
5. Start School Club.
6. Start Rent-a-Kite service.
7. Write a book about kites.
8. Write Kite Flying Guide.
9. Draw posters or murals.
10. Signs in school corridors.
11. Sponsor kite contest.
12. Invite kite maker to come.
13. Field trip to Japan.
14. Field trip to windy field.
15. Speech by Kite Store owner.
16. Hire a consultant.
17. Make taped directions with pictures.
18. Visit classes and give demonstrations.
19. Make learning centers to send to rooms.

Converge	I think #5, #8, #15, #17, and #19 look interesting. They're all things that I think we might actually be able to try.

SOLUTION-FINDING

Diverge-Criteria	1. Will anyone be interested? 2. Will I want to do it? 3. Will I be able to get materials? 4. Space? 5. Cost? 6. Time? 7. Teachers' permission? 8. Permission of Principal? 9. Any safety hazards? 10. Will I be able to do it alone? 11. Will it be fun? 12. Will kids learn anything?
Converge-Criteria	#1, #2, #11, and #12 seem important to me. I can take care of the others without too much fuss!
Converge-Ideas	I need to start working on Ideas #8 and #17 to be certain I really want to do this (writing a guide and making directions). Then we can talk with the Kite Shop owner (Idea #15) to review the material and help us improve it. We can work on Ideas #5 and #19 later if there's enough interest.

ACCEPTANCE-FINDING

Diverge	Possible steps: 1. Write down step-by-step Kite Making Directions 2. Make tape of directions. 3. List our illustrations and make sketches. 4. Make up a booklet. 5. Call person at Kite Shop. Possible problems: 1. Might miss some important steps. 2. What if there are errors in the guide? 3. No tape recorder. 4. Can't do the drawings accurately. 5. Kite Shop person won't help. 6. Other kids don't understand the Guide.
Converge	PLAN OF ACTION: 1. Get some books from Library and buy kite kit. 2. Read and study about kites on my own. 3. Get help from Kite Shop person on my own kites. 4. Make outline, organize step-by-step. 5. Write out step-by-step directions in detail. 6. Get an Art Student to help with illustrations. 7. Have Kite Shop person review material. 8. Have teachers review material and offer suggestions. 9. Try out materials with friends before making final draft. 10. Get permissions from teachers and principal for follow-up steps.

Creative Problem Solving: The Basic Course

SAMPLE CPS RUN-THROUGH: DEALING WITH A PERSONAL CONCERN

MESS-FINDING

Diverge — Some areas of personal interest or concern to me are:

1. Saving more money.
2. Finding more time for reading.
3. Not watching TV so much.
4. Sticking to my budget.
5. Losing about 20 pounds.
6. Helping friends who are fighting.
7. Brother and sister-in-law have new baby girl.

Converge — I'm always doing something about many of these–or putting them off. But #7 (the new baby in the family) is one that I want to do something about without delay!

DATA-FINDING

Diverge

WHO — Our family, brother & sister-in-law; baby; me.

WHAT — Money, gifts, visiting them soon, recognition of the new baby, want to do something personal and meaningful.

WHERE — Local stores? Baby shops? My apartment, their house.

WHEN — Soon! Within a week? My evenings and weekends are free, and theirs are usually free, too. Born a month ago.

WHY — My first Niece! I've always been close to them.
Must be inexpensive–my budget is very limited.
I've waited so long already–I feel guilty.

HOW — Quickly. Simply. Inexpensively. Elegantly. Meaningfully.
Show my pride, joy, love. Express congratulations.

Converge — What are V.I.D. (Very Important Data)?
  Inexpensive
  Express feelings
  Do something personal and meaningful
  Act promptly!

PROBLEM-FINDING

Diverge — In What Ways Might I (IWWMI . . .)
 . . . think of a personal gift for my brother and his family?
 . . . express my pride and joy for them?
 . . . express my happiness at this special time?
 . . . offer a personal gift for my new niece?
 . . . think of an unusual but appropriate gift?
 . . . not seem too cheap or forgetful?
 . . . find a gift that is personal but really special?
 . . . show my support and love for them?

Converge — To me, the one that really gets at the most important concern is:
IWWMI express my support and love for my brother and his family at this special time?

Creative Problem Solving: The Basic Course

IDEA-FINDING

Diverge
1. Help around the house.
2. Baby sit so they can go out.
3. Borrow money for a really expensive present.
4. Help care for the baby for a weekend.
5. Help fix up baby's room.
6. Buy books on parenting.
7. Buy story books to read to baby.
8. Clean house for them.
9. Get the baby a special gift.
10. Write a story or poem.
11. Take pictures of the baby.
12. Start a special scrapbook.
13. Do an oil painting of the baby.
14. Give them a Baby Album.

Converge

MOST PROMISING POSSIBILITIES seem to me to be:
- # 1 Help them around the house.
- # 2 Offer to babysit so they can go out by themselves.
- #12 Start a special scrapbook for them.

SOLUTION-FINDING

Diverge-Criteria
1. Low Cost
2. Easy to Do
3. Appropriate for Occasion
4. Can Do Quickly
5. Will they like it
6. Will it be "enough"
7. Will it add to their happiness
8. Will they be comfortable
9. Will I be comfortable

Converge-Criteria The most important criteria to me are #1, #2, #3, #4, #8, #9.

Converge-Ideas

IDEAS	1	2	3	4	8	9	Use	Hold	Reject
Help around house	E	G	G	E	G	F	X		
Offer to babysit	G	G	F	E	F	P		X	
Special Scrapbook	E	E	E	E	G	E	X		

E = Excellent; G = Good; F = Fair; P = Poor.

ACCEPTANCE-FINDING

Diverge

POSSIBLE ASSISTERS
1. I'll visit them this weekend.
2. Make the Scrapbook very personal.
3. Take some special pictures for the book when I visit.
4. Find some special cards and poems.
5. Enlist help of other relatives.

POSSIBLE RESISTERS
1. They might have other plans
2. They might already have an Album.
3. Can't find a suitable scrapbook that I can afford.

Converge

PLAN OF ACTION:
1. Call Brother and Sister-in-Law to arrange for weekend visit as soon as possible (perhaps this weekend).
2. Start search for suitable scrapbook immediately.
3. Call our other relatives and enlist their help and contributions.
4. Get film for my camera and have equipment ready to go.
5. Seek out unusual items to include in scrapbook.
6. Make up a special "Coupon Book" to give them for things I can do to help around the house—include things I'm sure I can do.
7. Begin assembling some pages of special items for the Scrapbook.

Creative Problem Solving: The Basic Course

SAMPLE CPS RUN-THROUGH: BUSINESS APPLICATIONS

MESS-FINDING WORKSHEET

Do you need to search for some MESSES?
  THINK ABOUT: People? Places? Plans? Processes? Products?
  CONSIDER: Strengths? Weaknesses? Hopes? Concerns?
  List some General Messes:

What are some OUTCOMES	• NEW SALES • MORE CLIENTS • BETTER INTERACTION WITH CLIENTS	• LEARNING SOME NEW SKILLS • EXPLORING LONG-RANGE TAX PLANNING
What possible Messes represent OBSTACLES?	• TOO MUCH WORK • TOO LITTLE TIME • SOME CLIENTS HAVE MOVED OUT OF AREA	• FINDING OUT WHAT TO DO FOR MR. + MRS. SMITH

From this general list of Messes, use the criteria for Ownership and Outlook to analyze the list and to select a Broad Goal on which to work:

Possible Messes	First Check For:			Then Use Outlook Criteria				Set Priority
	Influence	Interest	Imagination	Familiar?	Critical?	Immediate	Direction	
Increasing Sales	✓	✓	✓	✓	✓	✓	same	middle
Getting more clients	✓	no	✓	✓	no	no	same	low
Improved interaction	maybe	✓	✓	✓	helpful	no	worse	middle
Learn new skills	✓	✓	✓	maybe	helpful	✓	same	middle
Explore tax planning	✓	✓	✓	✓	no	✓	same	middle
Mr. + Mrs. Smith	✓	✓	✓	✓	very	✓	worse	high
Too much work	✓	no	✓	✓	no	no	same	low
Too little time	✓	✓	✓	✓	no	no	same	middle
Clients moved away	no	maybe	✓	no	no	no	got better	low

Creative Problem Solving: The Basic Course

DATA-FINDING WORKSHEET

Brief Description of Mess:

WORKING WITH MR. and MRS. SMITH

Enter data here – number each entry for convenience!

	KNOW:	✓VID	NEED/LIKE TO KNOW:	✓VID
WHO	(1) Mr. + Mrs. Smith (2) Me (5) Carpenter (3) My boss (4) Family members		(6) Who will do the remodeling?	
WHAT	(7) Remodel kitchen and dining area. (8) They also want to 'invest. (27) They need tax relief.		(9) Which do they value more? (19) What information should I send them?	
WHERE	(10) They live 500 miles away (11) We correspond regularly (12) Office (13) Their home		(14) Will they be coming into my area shortly? (15) Will I be going to their area shortly?	
WHEN	(16) They want to act soon! (17) I must respond soon!		(18) When's the best time to contact them?	
WHY	(20) To respond to their request. (21) To improve their finances (22) Earn a commission!			
HOW	(23) They have 20,000 to work with (26) They're in the 50% tax bracket		(24) Can they do the work themselves? (25) Are there other ways?	

Circle your "HITS" and Check the "Very Important Data" in the above list.

HOT SPOTS: Give Numbers: 1,2,3,4, 20,9,26   Name it: Knowing my clients
Give Numbers: 7,10,13, 23, 27   Name it: Needs and resources
Give Numbers: 16, 17, 10, 20   Name it: Managing the distance

PARAPHRASE – Express the Essence of the HOT SPOT that seems most important:

Determining the best course of action for their needs and resources.

Creative Problem Solving: The Basic Course

PROBLEM-FINDING WORKSHEET #1 (PF-1)

In What Ways Might (IWWM . . .) [How Might . . . or H^2 . . .]

WHO?	DO?	WHAT?
my clients	invest	according to existing plan
" "	remodel	without using savings
" "	clarify	their priorities
I	convince	them to follow plan
I	assist	clients meeting goals
I	improve	planning for their needs
We	agree	on a response
"	cooperate	for our mutual benefit

Now S-T-R-E-T-C-H for additional problem statements:

We	communicate	more effectively
We	reorganize	the plan
We	accomplish	the greatest benefits

Find the HOT SPOTS or clusters that seem to have IDEA-FINDING POTENTIAL:

Clients and I together   agree, cooperate   plan, course of action, goals

---

Which Problem Statement has most appeal for you to use for Idea-Finding?

IWWM my clients and I accomplish a new plan?

Is the statement you chose brief? Does it state the essense of your Mess? Is it a question for which you want ideas? Is it free of criteria?

Creative Problem Solving: The Basic Course

PROBLEM-FINDING WORKSHEET #2 (PF-2)
(For Key Word Variations)

What is your initial Problem Statement:

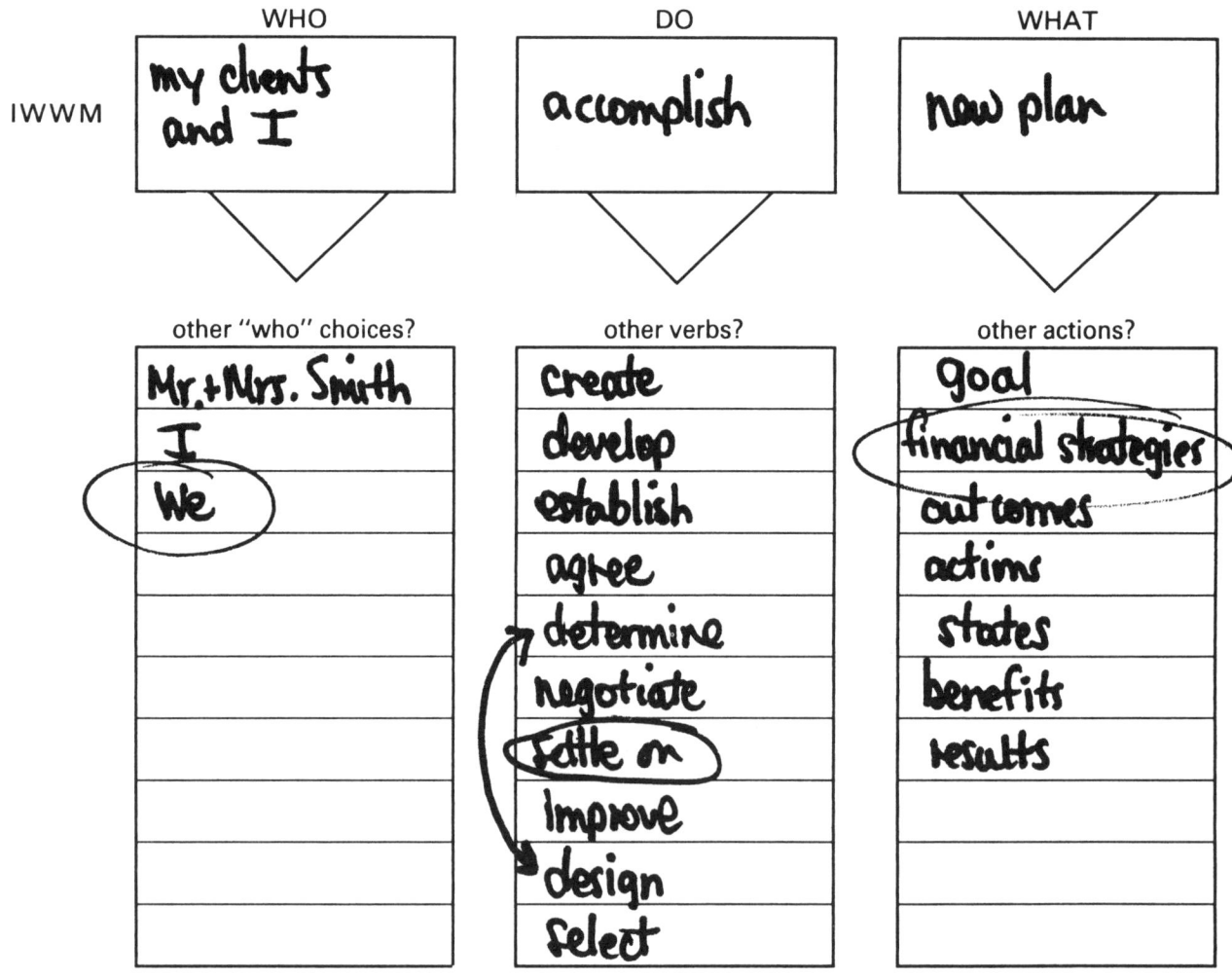

Test some combinations of one item from each of these three lists.

WRITE DOWN SOME NEW "HITS":

IWWM **we design and select financial strategies?**

Creative Problem Solving: The Basic Course

IDEA-FINDING WORKSHEET #1 (IF-1)

Brief Statement of Problem:

IWWM we design and select financial strategies?

IDEAS! IDEAS! IDEAS! IDEAS! IDEAS! and MORE IDEAS! . . . . .

1. Use interest as
2. write off
3. Make out a loan
4. for getting work done
5. Remodel and invest
6. the difference
7. Sell house and buy
8. a new one
9. Increase savings and
10. investment
11. Do it yourself re-
12. modeling
13. Do the remodeling
14. and use line of credit
15. Find investment that
16. pays for remodeling
17. Invest in a remodeling
18. company
19. Point out advantages
20. of investing
21. Show them other
22. similar cases
23. Write them up as a
24. case study for MONEY
25. MAGAZINE!
26.
27. Find high tax-relief
28. investments offering
29. decent return
30.
31. Have a remodeler
32. be a consultant in
33. the planning
34.
35. Decrease taxes
36.
37. Put off remodeling
38.
39. Increase yields and
40. earnings
41. Barter for the re-
42. modeling job
43.
44. Borrow from
45. relatives
46.
47. Find cheap home
48. improvement loan
49.
50.
51.
52.
53.
54.
55.
56.
57.
58.
59.
60.

Feel free to use more paper to think of even more IDEAS!

HOT SPOTS Numbers: _____ Name It: _____

Numbers: _____ Name It: _____

Numbers: _____ Name It: _____

Most Promising Possibilities (MPP) Are:

- Getting a remodeler in as a consultant to develop the plan
- Show tax benefits of investment plus remodeling loan

Creative Problem Solving: The Basic Course

SOLUTION-FINDING WORKSHEET #1 (SF-1)

STEP 1 GENERATE CRITERIA

What criteria should be used to screen, select, or support your most promising ideas?
Brainstorm for many possible criteria.
Then circle the criteria you decide to use.

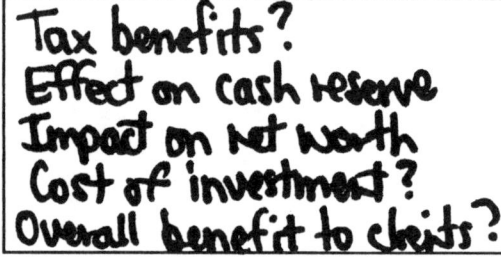

Tax benefits?
Effect on cash reserve
Impact on net worth
Cost of investment?
Overall benefit to clients?
Will clients be satisfied?
Risk of lost yield?
Risk of investment
Long range effect on goals?

STEP 2 SELECT YOUR METHOD

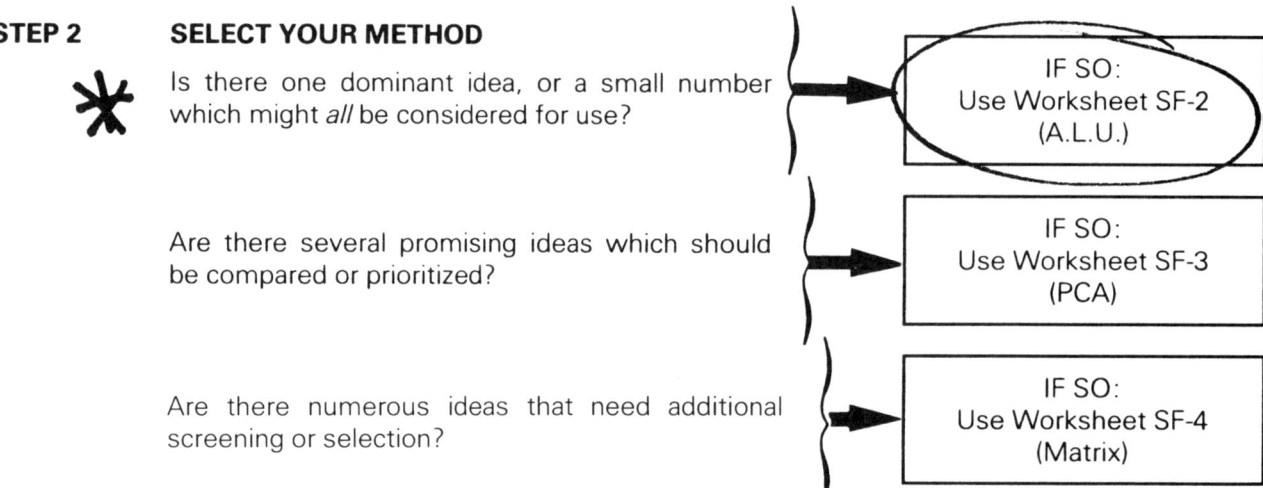

✱ Is there one dominant idea, or a small number which might *all* be considered for use? → **IF SO: Use Worksheet SF-2 (A.L.U.)** *(circled)*

Are there several promising ideas which should be compared or prioritized? → IF SO: Use Worksheet SF-3 (PCA)

Are there numerous ideas that need additional screening or selection? → IF SO: Use Worksheet SF-4 (Matrix)

STEP III PREPARE FOR ACCEPTANCE-FINDING

Summarize here the KEY POSSIBILITIES from Step II for which you will begin Acceptance-Finding:

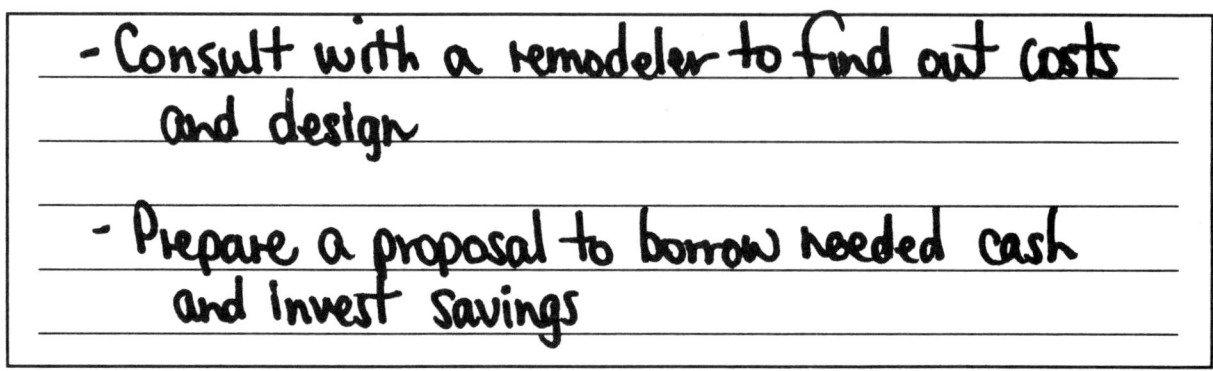

- Consult with a remodeler to find out costs and design

- Prepare a proposal to borrow needed cash and invest savings

164

Creative Problem Solving: The Basic Course

SOLUTION-FINDING WORKSHEET #2 (SF-2)

(Advantages - Limitations - Unique Ideas)

Even if you have only a few promising possibilities, all of which might be considered for use, it will still be helpful to examine them critically. Use the Criteria that you selected in SF Step I to help you consider the Advantages, Limitations and Unique Aspects for each promising possibility.

Promising Possibility #1: Get a remodeler as a consultant to develop the plan

Advantages:	Limitations:	Unique Aspects:
① We learn specific costs ② We become familiar with remodeling options ③ Helps get the remodeling done	① We look at only one thing: remodeling ② How do we know we chose the best remodeler?	- Could we find one who also provides home improvement loans? - The remodeler may help convince about need for financing work

Promising Possibility #2: Show tax benefits of investment plus remodeling loan

Advantages:	Limitations:	Unique Aspects:
They accumulate money They increase income They have tax benefits They still get remodeling done!	Must find a good loan rate	Not only can both be done, but by borrowing money, there is an additional tax write-off!!

Promising Possibility #3: _____

Advantages:	Limitations:	Unique Aspects:

RETURN TO STEP III OF SOLUTION-FINDING WORKSHEET #1)

ACCEPTANCE-FINDING WORKSHEET

ASSISTERS

Who/What will *assist* in implementing Ideas? Why do you need help? When and Where? How? How might you increase chances of success?

- A good remodeler
- My boss - Their tax status
- My secretary
- We have good leasing investment program (and real estate)

Of the ASSISTERS you've named, which ones are most likely to be involved? How will you enlist their help? Where? When? What if they can't?

- Use the investment program information to gather data about benefits.

RESISTERS

Who/What might resist or inhibit success? What might go wrong? What obstacles arise? What things might interfere with implementing?

- An over-anxious remodeler
- The distance between us
- * This may be more complex than simply spending money

Of the RESISTERS you've named, which ones are most likely to occur? How can it be prevented? What will you do if there *is* resistance of these kinds?

- Write a letter spelling out the options with a clear comparison and specific dollar amounts.

DEVELOP YOUR PLAN OF ACTION...

Step	Nature of Action Who? When? Where? Why? What? How?	Complete
24 HR.	Gather data from prospectus on real estate and leasing (see below)	☐
		☐
①	Write letter to clients	☐
②	Follow up with phone call	☐
③	Send paperwork	☐
option A	20,000 Cash Year 1 1,263	☐
	-15,000 Home Improvement 2 728	☐
	5,000 Available → 3 658	☐
	4 142	☐
	Saved in txs $2,791	☐
	plus 1,885 in tax sheltered cash flow	

166

Option Invest $20,000 and
B   use loan   Year 1   4,199
                           2,324
- Write off cost of   3,196
  loan   1,758
- Sell real estate and   11,477 Tax Savings
  equipment for about   5,713 Tax Shelters Cash Flow
  $20,000 in five years! 17,190

A COMPLETE CPS RUN-THROUGH OF YOUR OWN

Now that you have learned many of the basic methods of "tools" for the diverging and converging phases of the six CPS stages, and you have examined three brief run-through descriptions, it's time to work through the whole process using a problem of your own.

Since we will probably not be present in person to guide you through the process, we've developed some written materials that we hope will be helpful to you during this task:

1. *KEY QUESTIONS.* For each stage, you'll find a set of questions. These are the "key" questions to remind you about the major goal or focus of each phase. They're examples of the kinds of questions we would ask you in person, to help you remember what to do as you work through the process. They will help you focus your attention and direct your efforts towards the most essential aspects of each stage. Use these questions to be certain that you're really concentrating on the most important issues in each phase and stage.

2. *WORKSHEETS.* After each group of questions, you will find some worksheets (called "process flowsheets"). These will be helpful in organizing and maintaining a written record of your ideas and choices. For several of the stages, there will be more than one worksheet. You will not necessarily need to use each of these with every problem. We have included worksheets for several optional tools that can be used at your discretion.

Feel free to refer back to the previous chapters—especially *Chapters Three* through *Eight*—as you're working on your own problem. For this problem, try to use any methods and techniques to help you deal with the problem in original and meaningful ways.

At first, using the entire CPS process may seem very lengthy and exhausting. You'll discover, however, that the number and quality of ideas and plans you develop will easily be worth the time and effort. Eventually, many of these methods and techniques will become so familiar to you that it will seem "automatic" to use them during each new CPS opportunity. As your experience grows, so will your confidence and efficiency.

KEY QUESTIONS: MESS-FINDING

DIVERGENT

What's important to me? About what am I curious?
In what am I interested? About what am I concerned?
How do I plan? How do I approach things and situations?
How do I work with other people?
How do I react to new ideas and situations?
What kind of risk-taker am I?
What would I like to do, do more, or do better?
What's on my mind? What's nagging at me?
What's demanding my attention?
What have I been trying unsuccessfully to avoid?
What challenges and opportunities are on my mind?
What paradoxes and puzzling situations might I consider?

CONVERGENT

What demands are really most pressing?
What concerns are most urgent? Most important?
What will happen if I don't deal with these?
What risks are worth it? What risks are necessary?
What are my priorities?
What do I most hope to preserve, achieve, attain, or avoid?
What do I most want to expand, enhance, or improve?
What are my "bottom-line" goals and concerns?

MESS-FINDING WORKSHEET

Do you need to search for some MESSES?
 THINK ABOUT: People? Places? Plans? Processes? Products?
 CONSIDER: Strengths? Weaknesses? Hopes? Concerns?
 List some General Messes:

What are some OUTCOMES	
What possible Messes represent OBSTACLES?	

From this general list of Messes, use the criteria for Ownership and Outlook to analyze the list and to select a Broad Goal on which to work:

Possible Messes	First Check For:			Then Use Outlook Criteria				Set Priority
	Influence	Interest	Imagination	Familiar?	Critical?	Immediate	Direction	

KEY QUESTIONS: DATA-FINDING

DIVERGENT

Where can I get help?
What information do I have? Must I get? Would I like?
Who else is involved? To whom else should I talk?
What feelings, hunches, impressions, ideas, questions or observations might be involved?
What sources of information are available?
What might I read, watch, hear, see, study, learn?
What might I touch, taste, observe, feel, explore?
What might I have overlooked? What else?
What's already been tried? With what results?
When am I concerned? When is it on my mind? Where?
What is preventing me from doing what I want/need to do?
Why haven't I already solved this problem?
Why is this a concern or interest to me?
Has anyone else addressed this?
How can I get more information? Where? From what or whom?
Where might I look to find out more?

CONVERGENT

What data are most important to consider?
What "clusters" represent important themes or priorities?
What strands or issues run through all these data?
What's the real essence of this mess?
What patterns do I see in these data?
Which concerns are most important?
Which concerns might be grouped together?
What concerns or opportunities must be addressed first?
What data must be gathered before we proceed?

Creative Problem Solving: The Basic Course

DATA-FINDING WORKSHEET

Brief Description of Mess:

Enter data here – number each entry for convenience!

	KNOW:	√ VID	NEED/LIKE TO KNOW:	√ VID
WHO				
WHAT				
WHERE				
WHEN				
WHY				
HOW				

Circle your "HITS" and Check the "Very Important Data" in the above list.

HOT SPOTS: Give Numbers: _____ Name it: _____

Give Numbers: _____ Name it: _____

Give Numbers: _____ Name it: _____

PARAPHRASE – Express the Essense of the HOT SPOT that seems most important:

KEY QUESTIONS: PROBLEM-FINDING

DIVERGENT

What are some questions about which I would like more ideas?
What are some questions about which I would like different or varied ideas?
New and unusual ideas?
Why is this important to me? Why else?
What do I hope to attain, accomplish, gain, or resolve?
Why is this a problem for me?
What's *not* the problem?
How is this like or unlike other situations?
What do I really want to be able to do?
What would I like to produce or generate?
In what ways might I . . . (IWWMI . . .)
How might I . . . (HMI . . .)
How^2 do what? (H^2 . . .)

CONVERGENT

What's the question about which ideas are most needed?
Do some questions address similar themes or concerns?
What's the "common strand" among them?
What's the real problem?
What's the essence of my goals, objectives, or desires?
For what do I really want to search for possibilities?
On what question should I start working?
Where should my search begin?
What questions suggest the most useful directions?
Can I paraphrase the main issue in this situation? What is really my most important concern?

Creative Problem Solving: The Basic Course

PROBLEM-FINDING WORKSHEET #1 (PF-1)

In What Ways Might (IWWM . . .) [How Might . . . or H² . . .]

WHO?	DO?	WHAT?

Now S-T-R-E-T-C-H for additional problem statements:

Find the HOT SPOTS or clusters that seem to have IDEA-FINDING POTENTIAL:

Which Problem Statement has most appeal for you to use for Idea-Finding?

Is the statement you chose brief? Does it state the essense of your Mess? Is it a question for which you want ideas? Is it free of criteria?

174

Creative Problem Solving: The Basic Course

PROBLEM-FINDING WORKSHEET #2 (PF-2)
(For Key Word Variations)

What is your initial Problem Statement:

IWWM

WHO	DO	WHAT

other "who" choices?	other verbs?	other actions?

Test some combinations of one item from each of these three lists.

WRITE DOWN SOME NEW "HITS":

IWWM _____

Creative Problem Solving: The Basic Course

PROBLEM-FINDING WORKSHEET #3 (PF-3)
(For "Why" or "Why Else" Analysis)

ENTER YOUR INITIAL PROBLEM STATEMENT

> IWWM . . . _____
> _____
> _____

▼

> WHY?   Because_____
> _____
> _____

NEW PROBLEM STATEMENT ▼

> IWWM . . . _____
> _____
> _____

▼

> WHY?   Because_____
> _____
> _____

NEW PROBLEM STATEMENT ▼

> IWWM . . . _____
> _____
> _____

▼

> WHY?   Because_____
> _____
> _____

NEW PROBLEM STATEMENT ▼

> IWWM . . . _____
> _____
> _____

KEY QUESTIONS: IDEA-FINDING

DIVERGENT

What options and alternatives are there?
Can I think of more ways to do it?
Different Ways? New and unusual ways?
What would I do if there were no obstacles?
What's my greatest fantasy about how to do this?
How might this problem be solved?
What can be used or done in a new way?
What analogies might help? How do they work?
How many more possibilities can I create or generate?
Who else can offer some ideas?
What if the opposite were true?
What would I wish for in my wildest hopes and dreams?
Can I visualize or imagine solutions?
What new connections can I make?
How might I use some ideas or objects from a totally different context or purpose?

CONVERGENT

Which alternatives are most appealing? Attractive?
What ideas would I really like if I could make them work?
What options suggest new and promising ways to solve this problem?
What ideas do I really like best?
What ideas surprised me or caught my attention?
What ideas offered the most unusual or different perspective?
Do some of the ideas go together? Can they be combined, synthesized, or sequenced?
What ideas deserve closer examination or consideration?
What ideas offer you the best chance to do something?

Creative Problem Solving: The Basic Course

IDEA-FINDING WORKSHEET #1 (IF-1)

Brief Statement of Problem:

IDEAS!   IDEAS!   IDEAS!   IDEAS!   IDEAS!   and MORE IDEAS! . . . . .

1. _____   21. _____   41. _____
2. _____   22. _____   42. _____
3. _____   23. _____   43. _____
4. _____   24. _____   44. _____
5. _____   25. _____   45. _____
6. _____   26. _____   46. _____
7. _____   27. _____   47. _____
8. _____   28. _____   48. _____
9. _____   29. _____   49. _____
10. _____   30. _____   50. _____
11. _____   31. _____   51. _____
12. _____   32. _____   52. _____
13. _____   33. _____   53. _____
14. _____   34. _____   54. _____
15. _____   35. _____   55. _____
16. _____   36. _____   56. _____
17. _____   37. _____   57. _____
18. _____   38. _____   58. _____
19. _____   39. _____   59. _____
20. _____   40. _____   60. _____

Feel free to use more paper to think of even more IDEAS!

HOT SPOTS   Numbers: _____   Name It: _____

Numbers: _____   Name It: _____

Numbers: _____   Name It: _____

Most Promising Possibilities (MPP) Are:

IDEA-FINDING WORKSHEET #2 (IF-2)
(What If / Just Suppose)

Consider how many IDEAS you might be able to generate if you could simply wish away every obstacle or concern! Try it. Just say: "What if . . ." or "Just suppose . . ." and wipe away any concern. (What if cost were not a concern? What if time weren't limited? Just suppose the opposite were true?) Then, develop as many new ideas as you can.

WHAT IF_____?
Ideas:
_____   _____
_____   _____
_____   _____

WHAT IF_____?
Ideas:
_____   _____
_____   _____
_____   _____

WHAT IF_____?
Ideas:
_____   _____
_____   _____
_____   _____

JUST SUPPOSE THAT_____
Ideas:
_____   _____
_____   _____
_____   _____

JUST SUPPOSE THAT_____
Ideas:
_____   _____
_____   _____
_____   _____

JUST SUPPOSE THAT_____
Ideas:
_____   _____
_____   _____
_____   _____

CHECK FOR SOME NEW "HITS"

Creative Problem Solving: The Basic Course

IDEA-FINDING WORKSHEET #3 (IF-3)
(Scamper)

S - T - R - E - T - C - H for some new Ideas. Use SCAMPER to help:

KEY WORD(S)   NEW IDEAS:

S — substitute
others:

C — combine
others:

A — adapt
others:

M — modify
others:

P — put to other uses
others:

E — eliminate
others:

R — reverse, rearrange
others:

DON'T FORGET TO CHECK FOR YOUR "HITS!"

Creative Problem Solving: The Basic Course

IDEA-FINDING WORKSHEET #4 (IF-4)
(Attribute Listing)

What are some of the important ATTRIBUTES of your problem or situation?

What NEW IDEAS are suggested as you consider each ATTRIBUTE? S-T-R-E-T-C-H! What might you have overlooked before?

#1 _____

#2 _____

#3 _____

#4 _____

#5 _____

#6 _____

REMEMBER TO CHECK THESE IDEAS TO FIND SOME NEW "HITS"

Creative Problem Solving: The Basic Course

IDEA-FINDING WORKSHEET #5 (IF-5)
(Forced Relationships)

ARE YOU SEARCHING FOR SOME NEW AND UNUSUAL IDEAS?

Select 5 Objects At Random
(Use a newspaper, catalog, or phone book for ideas!)

What New Possibilities Might Each Object Suggest For Your Problem?

1.

2.

3.

4.

5.

REMEMBER TO LOOK OVER THE ENTIRE LIST . . .
CHECK THE "HITS"

KEY QUESTIONS: SOLUTION-FINDING

DIVERGENT

What factors or criteria might be considered?
What standards or "yardsticks" might be applied to these ideas?
How might we compare or analyze these ideas?
How might we determine the strengths and weaknesses of these ideas?
What factors might be most useful and important to consider in comparing, developing, modifying, or improving these ideas?
How might interesting ideas be made stronger or better?
How might fantasy ideas be made more realistic?
What makes some ideas less interesting or attractive?
Why are we pushed towards some ideas and away from others?
What new directions or concerns might be suggested?
What are the appealing features of all the ideas? How might these be combined or interchanged among ideas?

CONVERGENT

What criteria are most important and necessary to use?
Which criteria are essential? Desirable? Optional?
Which criteria will best help us to refine and develop ideas?

Using the Criteria . . .

How do these ideas measure up or compare?
Do the ideas satisfy needs and concerns? Meet priorities?
What ideas (or combinations) are most promising?
Which ones will really get the job done for me?
What ideas will get me to the goal?
What ideas might be most successful? Enjoyable? Rewarding?
Are the ideas complete? How do the criteria point to modifications or improvements?

Creative Problem Solving: The Basic Course

SOLUTION-FINDING WORKSHEET #1 (SF-1)

STEP 1 **GENERATE CRITERIA**

What criteria should be used to screen, select, or support your most promising ideas?
Brainstorm for many possible criteria.
Then circle the criteria you decide to use.

STEP 2 **SELECT YOUR METHOD**

Is there one dominant idea, or a small number which might *all* be considered for use?

IF SO:
Use Worksheet SF-2
(A.L.U.)

Are there several promising ideas which should be compared or prioritized?

IF SO:
Use Worksheet SF-3
(PCA)

Are there numerous ideas that need additional screening or selection?

IF SO:
Use Worksheet SF-4
(Matrix)

STEP III **PREPARE FOR ACCEPTANCE-FINDING**

Summarize here the KEY POSSIBILITIES from Step II for which you will begin Acceptance-Finding:

SOLUTION-FINDING WORKSHEET #2 (SF-2)
(Advantages - Limitations - Unique Ideas)

Even if you have only a few promising possibilities, all of which might be considered for use, it will still be helpful to examine them critically. Use the Criteria that you selected in SF Step I to help you consider the Advantages, Limitations and Unique Aspects for each promising possibility.

Promising Possibility #1: _____

Advantages:	Limitations:	Unique Aspects:
_____	_____	_____
_____	_____	_____
_____	_____	_____
_____	_____	_____

Promising Possibility #2: _____

Advantages:	Limitations:	Unique Aspects:
_____	_____	_____
_____	_____	_____
_____	_____	_____
_____	_____	_____

Promising Possibiltiy #3: _____

Advantages:	Limitations:	Unique Aspects:
_____	_____	_____
_____	_____	_____
_____	_____	_____
_____	_____	_____

RETURN TO STEP III OF SOLUTION-FINDING WORKSHEET #1)

Creative Problem Solving: The Basic Course

SOLUTION-FINDING WORKSHEET #3 (SF-3)
(Paired Comparison Analysis)

Use the PAIRED COMPARISON ANALYSIS when you have a small number of Promising Possibilities and you want to compare, rank, or prioritize them. (Directions for PCA will be found in Chapter VII.)

	B	C	D	E	F	G	H	I	Sum of Scores
A									A _____
B									B _____
C									C _____
D									D _____
E									E _____
F									F _____
G									G _____
H									H _____
I									I _____

1 - SLIGHTLY more important
2 - MODERATELY more important
3 - MUCH more important

Consider only the two ideas represented by each box formed by the intersection of the two axes of the grid. (*Example:* the left-most box on the top row is A&B, the box farthest to the right, A&I, the left-most box in the third row is C&D.)

1. Compare the two ideas represented by each box and decide which is more important in your opinion.
2. Place the letter corresponding to the more important idea in the box.
3. Using the scale at the left of the grid assign a weight (or degree of importance) to the letter . . . you are now saying how much more important one idea is over another.
4. Complete the grid by considering each box (pair of ideas) progressing from left to right and top to bottom.
5. Total the numerical scores received by each idea (letter) to obtain the raw weights of the idea (proportional weights may be derived by using the lowest score as one and calculating the rest). Use the horizontal and vertical rows labeled by the letter under consideration.

NEXT RETURN TO STEP III OF SOLUTION-FINDING WORKSHEET #1

SOLUTION-FINDING WORKSHEET #4 (SF-4)
(Idea Evaluation Matrix)

If you have many Promising Possibilities which must be "sorted" in order to screen or select the ones you want to continue to use, an Idea Evaluation Matrix can be helpful.

Enter the criteria you selected in Step I (SF Worksheet #1) in COLUMNS.
Enter the Most Promising Possibilities in the ROWS.
Select an Evaluation Scale (Excellent, Good, Fair, Poor; 1-5; etc.).
Taking one criterion at a time, evaluate all ideas systematically.
Analyze the results. (Remember to consider more than just total scores.)

Enter Your Most Promising Ideas M.P.P.	Enter Your Selected Criteria (Use Brief "Headlines")					Record Your Decisions			
						Use Now	Hold	Modify	Reject

THEN RETURN TO STEP III OF SOLUTION-FINDING WORKSHEET #1

KEY QUESTIONS: ACCEPTANCE-FINDING

DIVERGENT

How might we take these actions?
How might promising ideas be implemented?
What might be sources of assistance or resistance?
What might make action easier to take? More difficult?
What are some possible obstacles, objections, or concerns?
What might go right? So what?
What might go wrong? So what?
How might implementation problems be avoided?
What might we do if problems arise anyway?
What help might be needed? From whom? How obtained?
What might be the best thing that could happen?
What might be the worst thing that could occur?
What might stall, delay, or interfere with your plans?
Who or what could make your action a "breeze?"

CONVERGENT

What is most likely to help me implement my plan?
What's most likely to hinder successful implementation?
What specific actions are necessary?
    What should I do within 24 hours?
    What sequence of steps should be planned?
Who will help? How will their support be gained?
What resources are needed? Available? How obtained?
How do we start? Where? By when? What deadlines?
What timing and location factors must be considered?
Who *will* resist?
What are the most important steps to prevent problems?
What are the most likely contingent steps if problems arise?
How will we monitor and document progress?

Creative Problem Solving: The Basic Course

ACCEPTANCE-FINDING WORKSHEET

ASSISTERS

Who/What will *assist* in implementing Ideas? Why do you need help? When and Where? How? How might you increase chances of success?

RESISTERS

Who/What might resist or inhibit success? What might go wrong? What obstacles arise? What things might interfere with implementing?

Of the ASSISTERS you've named, which ones are most likely to be involved? How will you enlist their help? Where? When? What if they can't?

Of the RESISTERS you've named, which ones are most likely to occur? How can it be prevented? What will you do if there *is* resistance of these kinds?

DEVELOP YOUR PLAN OF ACTION . . .

Step	Nature of Action Who? When? Where? Why? What? How?	Complete
24 HR.		☐
		☐
		☐
		☐
		☐
		☐
		☐
		☐
		☐
		☐

CONTENDING WITH TIME PRESSURE: SNAP DECISION MAKING

Each time you use CPS to develop an effective Plan of Action for a new problem, you will become more confident in the effectiveness of the process, and in your own ability to use it successfully. You will probably also find that you will become more efficient, since, as you have more experience with many methods and techniques, they become easier to apply and demand less of your time and attention. That attention can be devoted increasingly to the content of the problem, as the process itself becomes easier and more comfortable. You'll move from one phase or stage to another smoothly and productively.

Even so, there will undoubtedly be many times when you will be called upon to take some action, to make a decision, or to develop and carry out a plan, under very demanding pressures or limitations. Commonly, for example, everyone must solve problems or take action under substantial time pressures. A decision must be made quite quickly, or a plan must be developed and implemented in a very brief time.[1] You might be tempted to think that you can't use CPS in those sudden, high-pressure situations. Even though you may not be able to do a formal, full-scale CPS run-through, your knowledge of CPS will still be very helpful. You can try, for example, to progress mentally from stage to stage, in a very streamlined or abbreviated manner, to increase your chances of creating a unique and productive view of the problem or solution. And when you feel at a loss–"stumped" for ideas, while the clock is ticking away–the methods and techniques you've learned for each stage, even used by themselves, can help you generate responses that will be at least better than you would have been able to do without them.

To assist you in your CPS efforts at such times, use the following procedure to practice with several sample problems.

1. Begin with Problem #1 in the list on this page. After reading the problem, allow yourself a maximum of *15 minutes* to develop a Plan of Action. As you work on the problem, remind yourself to use the six CPS stages by asking at least *one* Key Question for each phase.

2. Then read Problem #2 from the list. Try to do the same thing as you did in the previous step, but for this exercise, allow yourself only *10 minutes*. Try to pace yourself, to allow a few minutes for the "critical activity" in each stage.

3. Next, move to Problem #3. Allow yourself only *five minutes.*

4. The challenge is increasing! Work on Problem #4, allowing yourself this time only *three minutes.* Remember to try to include a concise, deliberate effort to use each stage of the process to guide your thinking.

5. The ultimate challenge: the *one minute CPS run-through!* Select any other problem from the list, and try to solve it in just *one minute.* You'll really need to "zip" through the stages in your mind!

Making Decisions Quickly and Creatively
"WHAT WOULD YOU DO? (W.W.Y.D.)"

1. You're stalled in a long line of snarled traffic that hasn't moved at all in twenty minutes. You're idly drumming your fingers on the steering wheel, when you accidentally started tapping the horn. Several sharp blasts escape before you realize it. The driver of the pick up truck in front of you opens his door, gets out, and starts to walk menacingly toward your car. He looks mean and unhappy. Your car is a convertible and the top is down. W.W.Y.D.?

2. You stop at the grocery store on the way home from the office, picking up several items you need for dinner and snacks for friends who are planning to visit you this evening. The checkout clerk says, "$19.75, please." When you open your wallet, you discover that you have only two dollars and a few pennies. A big sign over the register says, "Absolutely no checks or credit cards." The clerk is looking at you impatiently. W.W.Y.D.?

---

[1] The time needed for using CPS on a problem is related to many factors, including the importance and magnitude of the problem, the urgency of the situation, time and resources available, etc. You won't always have as much time as you'd like!

3. You've managed to get four tickets to the Big Game. After driving for an hour and a half, it's almost game time when you and your three friends finally park the car at the Stadium. You don't believe it could happen, but you've left the tickets home on your desk, and no one else is home. W.W.Y.D.?

4. To broaden your cultural horizons, you've enrolled in an Art Appreciation course. Tonight's class involves a tour of the local gallery. You spot a large canvas that's really ugly, and you make a few pointed comments about it. When you get closer to the painting, you see the artist's name. The painting was done by the class instructor, who has been standing right next to you. It's too late to get a refund on your tuition, and you're certain the instructor heard your comments. W.W.Y.D.?

5. On a campaign trip in the "deep woods," you and your partner are awakened in the middle of the night by rustling in the bushes and growling sounds outside your tent. You do not have any weapons. It's pitch dark outside, but it sounds like a wild dog or perhaps even a bear. W.W.Y.D.?

6. Visiting a large city for the first time, you and a friend decide to get to know the town by using the subway system. On the way back to your hotel late at night, you find yourself lost. You exit at the last stop, a far away station in a very unpleasant and run-down area. The subway system is closing until 6:30 AM. The only sign of life in the area is a small tavern. There are several motorcycles parked outside, and from inside, you hear curses, shouting, and loud, drunken challenges. W.W.Y.D.?

7. As the supervisor of a small group of employees in your organization, you've developed a hard-working and close-knit group. You've been assigned a new person, fresh from college. He is surly, over-confident, uncooperative, usually in need of a shower, and antagonistic to everyone in the group. But he *is* the only son of the Big Boss. W.W.Y.D.?

8. You're ready to begin your big vacation trip with your spouse. After an exhausting, all day flight, you arrive at a luxurious, isolated island resort. The clerk informs you that no reservation in your name can be found in their computer. You don't have a confirmation slip. The desk clerk insists that every room in the hotel is booked solid for the week because of a large convention. There are no other hotels on the island. W.W.Y.D.?

IS THE ENTIRE CPS PROCESS ALWAYS NECESSARY?

Most of the time, it is important to give at least some deliberate attention to all of the CPS stages when solving a problem. There may be some situations, however, in which it could be beneficial to use only a selected portion of the process.

Review the Process Decision Matrix to help you decide where to begin in your work on a particular problem or challenge. Begin by checking Column A, to determine the level at which you're starting. Then proceed to Column B, to verify your earliest point of *uncertainty* about the situation. Then look at the corresponding line in Column C, to determine your probable starting point in the process.

Process Decision Matrix

A If you're certain about:	B But unsure about:	C Consider:
A general area of concern, broad goal, or general opportunity.	What data are involved and which are most essential.	Reviewing M-F briefly but then starting at D-F.
A general goal, and explicit list of data involved in the situation.	Nature of the "real" or most important problem area.	Reviewing M-F & D-F briefly but then starting at P-F.
A question for which you want to get some new ideas.	The ideas that might answer the question.	Using IWWMI or H^2 and starting at I-F.
A problem statement and several new ideas for it.	Ways to select and develop the most promising ideas.	"Stretching" for ideas, then starting at S-F.
The most promising ideas for a specific problem statement.	How to implement the ideas as successfully as possible.	Reviewing criteria for evaluating the ideas, then beginning at A-F.
An intended Plan of Action.	Implementing the steps successfully.	Beginning with a try-out or "pilot" but have other alternatives ready. (Make it a new *Mess.*)

CPS PROCESS SUMMARY

To help you remember your key steps or tasks in each stage of CPS, we have prepared a brief summary.

- In every stage:

    1. Remember to follow the ground rules for diverging and converging.
    2. Write down your ideas!
    3. Don't be afraid to experiment with new techniques.

- Mess-Finding:

    1. Remember that different members of a group will approach problems in various ways.
    2. Individuals use their unique learning styles to define and work on problems.
    3. Be alert to obstacles or blocks to your creative problem solving efforts.
    4. Problem solving is more effective when you use a specific process or method.
    5. Messes should be stated in a way that's *broad, brief,* and *beneficial.*

6. Ownerhsip is essential; check for *influence, interest,* and *imagination.*

7. Remember to check your specific outlook, by checking for *familiarity, critical nature, immediacy,* and *direction.*

- **Data-Finding:**

    1. Remember to search for data from many perspectives; consider *information, impressions, observations, feelings,* and *questions.*

    2. Ask: Who? What? When? Where? Why? and How?

    3. Make a note of Very Important Data (VID).

    4. Look for Hits and Hot Spots.

    5. Use *paraphrasing* to locate and describe the essential components of the Mess.

    6. Set *priorities* for various components within the Mess.

- **Problem-Finding:**

    1. Begin with the most promising areas from Data-Finding.

    2. Use a stem that invites ideas (IWWMI/H^2/HMI . . .).

    3. Look for questions with *Idea-Finding potential.*

    4. Express the ownership and the goal clearly.

    5. Use verbs that emphasize *action.*

    6. Good problem statements are concise and free of criteria.

    7. Use *Why/Why Else* to go up the ladder of abstraction.

    8. Use *Key Word Variations* to consider sub-problems.

    9. Find Hits and Hot Spots to help you prioritize and select an effective problem statement.

- **Idea-Finding:**

    1. Strive for many, varied, and unusual ideas.

    2. Stretch your thinking by using many idea-generating tools. Don't be content with just a few ideas.

    3. Don't overlook the need for incubation.

    4. Look for new and unusual ideas by using idea checklists (such as SCAMPER), attribute listing, forced relationships, or morphological analysis.

    5. Look for your Most Promising Possibilities (MPP).

- **Solution Finding:**

    1. Generate many criteria to help you *screen, select,* and *support* promising ideas.

    2. Select an appropriate scale for weighing or analyzing your ideas.

    3. Use A-L-U (Advantages-Limitations-Unique Connections) to analyze promising possibilities in detail.

    4. Use PCA (Paired Comparison Analysis) to compare, rank, or prioritize several promising possibilities.

5. Use an *Idea Evaluation Matrix* to screen, select, or evaluate many ideas using specific criteria.

6. Look critically at promising ideas to prepare for implementation in Acceptance-Finding.

- Acceptance-Finding:

    1. Consider many possible sources of *assistance* (people, places, things, events, resources, etc.) to help you insure successful implementation.

    2. Consider many possible sources of *resistance* that might inhibit or interfere with successful implementation.

    3. Plan specific ways to use *assisters* and prevent or overcome *resisters*.

    4. Use specific criteria to select major areas of concern.

    5. Use *Imaging for Success* procedures.

    6. Establish a specific *Plan of Action,* including an immediate or 24 hour step, short term actions, and long range plans; include alternatives or contingencies.

    7. Troublesome areas may serve as new Messes for recycling the entire CPS process.

APPENDIX A

APPENDIX A: CPS RESOURCES

To Learn More About CPS

If studying *Creative Problem Solving: the Basic Course* has whetted your appetite, and you're anxious to learn more about CPS and its uses, here are some suggestions that might be helpful.

Reading

The literature on creativity has grown rapidly since Guilford's Presidential address to the American Psychological Association in 1950, during which he reported the neglect of the study of creativity and the scarcity of the subject in the literature. In his review of the Annual Index of *Psychological Abstracts*, for the 23 years it was in existence prior to 1950, only 186 entries from a total of 121,000 dealt with creativity. That was less than two-tenths of one percent of the books and articles indexed!

Using the topics Guilford used, we found over 5,600 references to creativity in *Psychological Abstracts* as of June, 1984. This search covered the period from 1967 to the present. Creativity-related entries now represented 1.3% of the 418,000 total citations in the Abstracts for that period. Although still only a small segment of the literature of psychology, it is quite clear that publications about creativity have increased substantially.

Another way of illustrating the extent of reading material available on creativity is to point out that a special collection on creativity has been established in a university library (at the Butler Library at the State University College at Buffalo, New York). In this collection alone, there are over 3000 books and 2000 theses and dissertations. There are also numerous other private library collections specifically concerned with creativity, innovation, leadership, and problem solving.

The following list of books has been selected to provide you a starting point for readings on:
- general analyses of the nature and nurture of creativity;
- other creative problem solving techniques and processes;
- applications of creativity in education and training;
- applications of creativity and innovation in organizations;
- bibliographic resources on creativity.

Books

A. **General Reading on the Nature and Nurture of Creativity:**

Amabile, T. M. *The social psychology of creativity.* New York: Springer-Verlag, 1983.
Anderson, H. H. *Creativity and its cultivation.* New York: Harper and Brothers, 1959.
Ainsworth-Land, G. & V. *Forward to basics.* Buffalo, NY: DOK, 1982.
Arieti, S. *Creativity: The magic synthesis.* New York: Basic Books, 1976.
Austin, J. H. *Chance, chase and creativity: The lucky art of novelty.* New York: Columbia University Press, 1977.
Barnes, L. *The creative imagination.* London: Allen & Unwin, 1960.
Barron, F. *Creative person and creative process.* New York: Holt, Rinehart, 1969.
Biondi, A. M. *The creative process.* Buffalo, NY: DOK, 1972.
Bruch, C., Butterfield, S. M., Gowan, J. C., Hall, L. K., Olson, M., Parnes, S. J., Preston, J., Taylor, C. W., Torrance, E. P. & Wolf, M. H. *The faces and forms of creativity.* Ventura, CA: Ventura County Superintendent of Schools Office (N/S, LTI), 1981.
Crawford, R. P. *Think for yourself.* Wells, VT: Fraser Publishing Company, 1973.
Davis, G. *Creativity is forever.* Cross Plains, WI: Badger Press, 1981.
Davis, G. *Psychology of problem-solving.* New York: Basic Books, 1973.
deBono, E. *Lateral thinking: A textbook of creativity.* New York: Pelican, 1977.
Dewey, J. *How we think.* Lexington, MA: D. C. Heath and Company, 1933.
Dutton, D. & Krausz, M. *The concept of creativity in science and art.* Boston, MA: Dist. for US & Can. by Kluwer, 1981.
Eisner, E. *Think with me about creativity.* Dansville, NY: F. A. Owen, 1964.
Gardner, H. *Art, mind and brain: A cognitive approach to creativity.* New York: Basic Books, 1982.
Gowan, J. C. *Development of the creative individual.* San Diego, CA: Robert R. Knapp, 1972.

Getzels, J. W. & Csikszentmihalyi, M. *The creative vision: A longitudinal study of problem finding in art.* New York: John Wiley & Sons, 1976.

Getzels, J. W. & Jackson, P. W. *Creativity and intelligence: Explorations with gifted students.* New York: John Wiley & Sons, 1962.

Ghiselin, B. *The creative process,* New York: Mentor Books, 1952.

Goertzel, M. G., Goertzel, V. & Goertzel, I. G. *300 eminent personalities: A psychosocial analysis of the famous.* San Francisco, CA: Jossey-Bass Publishers, 1978.

Guilford, J. P. *Way beyond the I.Q.: Guide to improving intelligence and creativity.* Buffalo, NY: Creative Education Foundation and Creative Synergetic Associates, 1977.

Guilford, J. P. *The nature of human intelligence.* New York: McGraw-Hill, 1967.

Gruber, H. E., Terrell, G. & Wertheimer, M. (eds.) *Contemporary approaches to creative thinking: A symposium held at the University of Colorado.* New York: Atherton Press, 1967.

Hampden-Turner, C. *Maps of the mind: Charts and concepts of the mind and its labyrinths.* New York: Collier Books, 1981.

Hausman, C. R. *A discourse on novelty and creation.* Albany, NY: State University of New York Press, 1984.

Holsinger, R., Jordan C. & Levenson, L. *The creative encounter.* Glenview, IL: Scott, Foresman and Co., 1971.

Janis, I. L. & Mann, L. *Decision making: A psychological analysis of conflict, choice and commitment.* New York: The Free Press, 1977.

Judson, H. F. *The search for solutions.* New York: Holt, Rinehart and Winston, 1980.

Kneller, G. F. *The art and science of creativity.* New York: Holt, Rinehart and Winston, 1965.

Khatena, J. *Imagery and creative imagination.* Buffalo, New York: Bearly Limited, 1984.

Koestler, A. *The act of creation,* New York: Macmillan, 1969.

MacKinnon, D. W. *In search of human effectiveness: Identifying and developing creativity.* Buffalo, New York: Creative Education Foundation and Creative Synergetic Associates, 1978.

Mansfield, R. S. & Busse, T. U. *The psychology of creativity and discovery: Scientists and their work.* Chicago: Nelson-Hall, 1981.

Maslow, A. *The farther reaches of human nature.* New York: Viking Press, 1974.

May, R. *The courage to create.* New York: Norton, 1975.

Mooney, R. L. & Razik, T. A. (eds.) *Explorations in creativity,* New York: Harper and Row, 1967.

Osborn, A. F. *Applied imagination: Principles and procedures of creative problem-solving.* New York: Charles Scribner's Sons, 1963.

Parnes, S. J. *The magic of your mind,* Buffalo, New York: Creative Education Foundation and Bearly Limited, 1981.

Parnes, S. J. & Harding, H. F. *A source book for creative thinking,* New York: Charles Scribner's Sons, 1962.

Perkins, D. N. *The mind's best work: A new psychology of creative thinking.* Cambridge, MA: Harvard University Press, 1981.

Polya, G. *How to solve it: A new aspect of mathematical method.* Princeton, NJ: Princeton University Press, 1973.

Prince, G. M. *The practice of creativity: A manual for dynamic group problem-solving.* New York: Harper & Row, 1970.

Rossman, J. *The psychology of the inventor.* Washington: Inventors Publishing, 1931.

Rothenberg, A. & Hausman, C. R. *The creativity question,* Durham, NC: Duke University Press, 1976.

Rothenberg, A. *The emerging goddess: The creative process in art, science and other fields,* Chicago, IL: The University of Chicago Press, 1979.

Rugg, H. *Imagination.* New York: Harper and Row, 1963.

Simonton, D. K. *Genius, creativity and leadership.* MA: Harvard University Press, 1984.

Stein, M. I. & Heinze, S. J. *Creativity and the individual.* Glencoe, IL: The Free Press, 1960.

Stein, M. I. *Stimulating creativity: Volume I and II.* New York: Academic Press, 1974.

Tart, C. *Altered states of consciousness.* New York: Wiley, 1969.

Taylor, C. W. *Creativity: Progress and potential.* New York: McGraw-Hill, 1964.

Taylor, C. W. *Widening horizons in creativity: The proceedings of the fifth Utah creativity research conference.* New York: Wiley, 1964.

Taylor, C. W. & Barron, F. (eds.) *Scientific creativity: Its recognition and development.* New York: Wiley, 1973.

Taylor, I. A. & Getzels, J. W. (eds.) *Perspectives in creativity.* Chicago, IL: Aldine Publishing Co., 1975.

Torrance, E. P. *The search for satori and creativity.* Buffalo, NY: Creative Education Foundation and Creative Synergetic Associates, 1979.

Treffinger, D. J., Isaksen, S. G. & Firestien, R. L. *Handbook of creative learning: Volume one.* Williamsville, NY: Center for Creative Learning, 1982.

Ungson, G. R. & Braunstein, D. N. *Decision making: An interdisciplinary inquiry.* Boston, MA: Kent Publishing, 1982.

Vernon, P. E. (ed.) *Creativity: Selected readings.* New York: Penguin Books, 1970.

Wallas, G. *The art of thought.* New York: Harcourt Brace and Company, 1926.

Walter, G. A. & Marks, S. E. *Experiential learning and change: Theory, design and practice.* Somerset, NJ: Wiley, 1981.

Wertheimer, M. *Productive Thinking.* New York: Harper and Brothers, 1945.

Wickelgren, W. A. *How to solve problems: Elements of a theory of problems and problem solving.* San Francisco, CA: W. H. Freeman, 1974.

B. **Other Creative Problem-Solving Techniques and Processes:**

Allen, M. *Morphological creativity.* Englewood Cliffs, NJ: Prentice-Hall, 1962.
Biondi, A. M. (ed.) *Have an affair with your mind.* Great Neck, NY: Creative Synergetic Associates, 1974.
Crawford, R. *Direct creativity with attribute listing.* Wells, VT: Fraser, 1964.
Davis, G. & Scott, J. (eds.) *Training creative thinking.* New York: Holt, Rinehart and Winston, 1971.
deBono, E. *The CORT thinking skills program.* New York: Pergamon Press, 1984.
Delbecq, A., Van de Ven, A. & Gustafson, D. *Group techniques for program planning: A guide to nominal group and delphi processes.* Glenview, IL: Scott, Foresman & Co., 1975.
Gordon, W. J. J. & Poze, T. *The metaphorical way of learning and knowing: Applying synectics to sensitivity and learning situations.* Cambridge, MA: Porpoise Books, 1973.
Gordon, W. *Synectics.* New York: Harper and Row, 1961.
Gordon, W. & Poze, T. *The basic course in synectics.* Cambridge, MA: Porpoise Books, 1981.
Gordon, W. & Poze, T. *The new art of the possible.* Cambridge, MA: Porpoise Books, 1980.
Kepner, C. & Tregoe, B. *The new rational manager.* Princeton, NJ: Princeton Research Press, 1981.
McKim, R. H. *Thinking visually: A strategy manual for problem solving.* Belmont, CA: Lifetime Learning Publications, 1980.
Prince, G. *The practice of creativity.* New York: Harper and Row, 1970.
Raudsepp, E. *Creative growth games.* New York: Perigree Books/G. P. Putnam's Sons, 1977.
Raudsepp, E. *More creative growth games.* New York: Perigree Books/G. P. Putnam's Sons, 1980.
Raudsepp, E. *How creative are you?* New York: Perigree Books/G. P. Putnam's Sons, 1981.
Upton, A. *Design for thinking: A first book in semantics.* Palo Alto, CA: Pacific Books, 1961.
Upton, A., Sampon, R. & Farmer, A. *Creative analysis.* New York: Dutton, 1978.
Van Gundy, A. B. *108 ways to get a bright idea and increase your creative potential.* Englewood Cliffs, NJ: Prentice-Hall, 1983.
Zwicky, F. *Discovery, invention, research through the morphological approach.* New York: MacMillan, 1969.

C. **Applications of Creativity in Education and Training:**

Aschner, M. J. & Bish, C. E. *Productive thinking in education.* Washington, DC: National Education Association, 1965.
Bingham, A. *Improving children's facility in problem solving.* New York: Columbia Teacher's College, 1958.
Bleedhorn, B. D. *Looking ahead: Tested ideas in future studies.* Buffalo, NY: DOK, 1981.
Brand, L. *Home style learning.* Englewood Cliffs, NJ: Prentice Hall, 1981.
Bruner, J. *Beyond the information given.* New York: Norton, 1973.
Burns, M. *The book of think or how to solve a problem twice your size.* Boston, MA: Little, Brown and Co., 1976.
Callahan, C. M. *Developing creativity in the gifted and talented.* Reston, VA: The Council for Exceptional Children, 1978.
Cole, H. *Process education.* Englewood Cliffs, NJ: Educational Technology Publications, 1972.
Covington, M. V. *The productive thinking program: A course in learning to think.* Ohio: Charles E. Merill Publishing Co., 1972.
deBono, E. *Eureka: An illustrated history of inventions from the wheel to the computer.* New York: Holt, Rinehart and Winston, 1974.
deBono, E. *Teaching thinking.* New York: Penguin Books, 1980.
deBono, E. *Think links.* Blandford Forum, Dorset, UK: Direct Education Services, Ltd., 1976.
Dembo, M. *Teaching for learning: Applying educational psychology in the classroom.* New York: Scott, Foresman and Co., 1981.
Duling, G. A. *Creative problem-solving for an eency weency spider.* Buffalo, NY: DOK, 1983.
Duling, G. A. *Creative problem-solving for the fourth little pig.* Buffalo, NY: DOK, 1984.
Eberle, R. F. *Chip in: Motivational activities to stimulate better thinking.* Carthage, IL: Good Apple, 1982.
Eberle, R. F. *Help! In solving problems creatively at home and school.* Carthage, IL: Good Apple, 1984.
Eberle, R. F. *SCAMPER.* Buffalo, NY: DOK, 1971.
Eberle, R. F. *Scamper on.* Bufflao, NY: DOK, 1984.
Eberle, R. F. *Visual thinking: A scamper tool for useful imaging.* Buffalo, NY: DOK, 1982.
Eberle, R. F. & Stanish, R. *CPS for kids: A resource book for teaching creative problem-solving to children.* Buffalo, NY: DOK, 1980.
Feldhusen, J. F. & Treffinger, D. J. *Creative thinking and problem solving in gifted education.* Dubuque, IA: Kendall/Hunt Publishing Company, 1980.
Foster, J. *Creativity and the teacher.* London: MacMillan, 1971.
Gallagher, Jr. *Teaching the gifted child.* Boston, MA: Allyn and Bacon, 1975.
Guilford, J. P. *Intelligence, creativity, and their educational implications.* San Diego, CA: Robert R. Knapp, 1968.
Goodwin, P. *Future world.* New York: Crescent Books, 1979.
Gordon, W. J. J. & Poze, T. *Activities in metaphor.* Cambridge, MA: Porpoise Books, 1973.
Gordon, W. J. J. & Poze, T. *Appreciating literature from the inside.* Cambridge, MA: Porpoise Books, 1974.
Gordon, W. J. J. & Poze, T. *Strange and familiar book III - Elementary.* Cambridge, MA: Porpoise Books, 1975.
Gordon, W. J. J. & Poze, T. *Teaching is listening.* Cambridge, MA: Porpoise Books, 1972.
Gowan, J. C., Khatena, J. & Torrance, E. P. *Creativity: Its educational implications.* 2nd ed. Dubuque, IA: Kendall/Hunt Publishing Company, 1981.

Greer, M. & Rubinstein, B. *Will the real teacher please stand up?* Santa Monica, CA: Goodyear Publishing Co., 1978.

Humphreys, A., Post, T. & Ellis, A. *Interdisciplinary methods: A thematic approach.* Santa Monica, CA: Goodyear Publishing Company, 1981.

Johnson, D. W. & Johnson, R. T. *Learning together and alone.* Englewood Cliffs, NJ: Prentice-Hall, 1975.

Johnson, D. W., Johnson, R. T., Holubee, E. & Roy, P. *Circles of learning: Cooperation in the classroom.* Washington, D.C.: Association for Supervision and Curriculum Development, 1984.

Joyce, B. & Weil, M. *Models of teaching.* Englewood Cliffs, NJ: Prentice-Hall, 1980.

Kaplan, S. N., Kaplan, J. B., Madsen, S. K. & Gould, B. T. *Change for children.* Pacific Palisades, CA: Goodyear Publishing Co., 1973.

Keller, C. *The best of Rube Goldberg.* Englewood Cliffs, NJ: Prentice-Hall, 1979.

Khatena, J. *The creatively gifted child: Suggestions for parents and teachers.* New York: Vantage Press, 1978.

Koberg, D. & Bagnall, J. *The universal traveler.* Los Altos, CA: William Kaufmann, Inc., 1974.

Maker, C. J. *Teaching models in education of the gifted.* Rockville, MD: Aspen Systems Corporation, 1982.

Maker, C. J. *Curriculum development for the gifted.* Rockville, MD: Aspen Systems Corporation, 1982.

Massialas, B. & Zevin, J. *Creative encounters in the classroom: Teaching and learning through discovery.* New York: Wiley, 1967.

McCollum J. *Ah hah! The inquiry process of generating and testing knowledge.* Santa Monica, CA: Goodyear Publishing Company, 1978.

Mohan, M. & Laspada, S. *Mind-stimulating activities,* Buffalo, NY: DOK, 1979.

Murphy, J. *Weird and wacky inventions.* New York: Crown Publishers, 1978.

Noller, R. B. *Scratching the surface of creative problem-solving: A bird's eye view of CPS.* Buffalo, NY: DOK, 1977.

Noller, R. B., Parnes, S. J. & Biondi, A. M. *Creative actionbook.* NY: Charles Scribner's Sons, 1977.

Noller, R. B., Treffinger, D. J. & Houseman, E. D. *It's a gas to be gifted or CPS for the gifted and talented.* Buffalo, NY: DOK, 1979.

Noller, R. B., Heintz, R. E. & Blaeuer, D. A. *Creative problem solving in mathematics.* Buffalo, NY: DOK, 1978.

Parnes, S. J., Noller, R. B. & Biondi, A. M. *Guide to creative action.* New York: Charles Scribner's Sons, 1977.

Raths, L. E., Wasserman, S., Jonas, A. & Rothstein, A. M. *Teaching for thinking: Theory and application.* Columbus, OH: Charles E. Merrill Publishing Co., 1967.

Renzulli, J. *New directions in creativity* (Five Volumes: Mark A, Mark B, Mark 1, Mark 2, Mark 3). New York: Harper and Row, 1976.

Ricca, J. R. & Treffinger, D. J. *Adventures in creative thinking: From the classroom to home and back again.* Buffalo, NY: DOK, 1982.

Roper, A. & Harvey, L. *The pattern factory: Elementary problem-solving through patterning.* CA: Creative Publications, 1980.

Shallcross, D. J. *Teaching creative behavior: How to evoke creativity in children of all ages.* Englewood Cliffs, NJ: Prentice-Hall, 1981.

Shallcross, D. J. & Sisk, D. *The growing person: How to encourage healthy emotional development in children.* Englewood Cliffs, NJ: Prentice-Hall, 1982.

Shears, L. M. & Bower, E. M. (eds.) *Games in education and development.* Springfield, IL: Charles C. Thomas, 1974.

Smith, J. *Setting conditions for creative thinking in the elementary school.* Boston: Allyn and Bacon, 1969.

Stanish, R. *Hippogriff feathers: Encounters with creative thinking.* Carthage, IL: Good Apple, 1981.

Stanish, R. *The unconventional invention book: Classroom activities for activating student inventiveness.* Carthage, IL: Good Apple, 1981.

Sund, R. B. & Carin, A. *Creative questioning and sensitive listening techniques.* Columbus, OH: Charles E. Merrill Publishing Co., 1978.

Taylor, C. W. *Igniting creative potential.* Salt Lake City, UT: Project IMPLODE (P.L. 90-247 ESEA), 1971.

Torrance, E. P. & Myers, R. E. *Creative learning and teaching.* New York: Dodd, Mead and Company, 1970.

Torrance, E. P. *Guiding creative talent.* Englewood Cliffs, NJ: Prentice-Hall, 1962.

Treffinger, D. J. *Encouraging creative learning for the gifted and talented: A handbook of methods and techniques.* Ventura, CA: Ventura County Superintendent of Schools Office, 1980.

Wallach, M. & Kogan, N. *Modes of thinking in young children.* New York: Holt, Rinehart and Winston, 1966.

Weinstein, M. & Goodman, J. *Playfair.* San Luis Obispo, CA: Impact Publishers, 1980.

Whitehead, A. N. *The aims of education.* New York: The New American Library, 1929.

Williams, F. E. *The second volume of classroom ideas for encouraging thinking and feeling.* Buffalo, NY: DOK, 1982.

Williams, F. E. *Classroom ideas for encouraging thinking and feeling,* 2nd ed., Buffalo, NY: DOK, 1970.

Wittmer, J. & Myrick, R. *Facilitative teaching.* Pacific Palisades, CA: Goodyear Publishing Co., 1974.

D. Applications of Creativity and Innovation in Organizations:

Adams, Jr. *Conceptual blockbusting.* Stanford, CA: Stanford Alumni Association, 1974.

Albrecht, J. *Brain power: Learn to improve your thinking skills.* Englewood Cliffs, NJ: Prentice-Hall, 1980.

Anthony, W. P. *Participative management.* Reading, MA: Addison-Wesley Publishing Co., 1978.

Argyris, C. *Increasing leadership effectiveness.* New York: Wiley, 1976.

Astin, A. W. *Maximizing leadership effectiveness.* San Francisco, CA: Jossey Bass, 1980.

Bass, B. M. *Stogdill's handbook of leadership: A survey of theory and research.* New York: The Free Press, 1981.

Bennis, W. G., Benne, K. D. & Corey, J. E. *The planning of change,* 3rd ed. New York: Holt, Rinehart and Winston, 1976.
Bertcher, H. *Group participation: Techniques for leaders and members.* Beverly Hills, CA: SAGE, 1979.
Bertcher, H. & Maple, F. *Creating groups.* Beverly Hills, CA: SAGE, 1977.
Bradford, L. P. *Making meetings work: A guide for leaders and group members.* San Diego, CA: University Associates, 1976.
Brighman, H. J. *Problem solving: A logical and creative approach.* Atlanta, GA: Georgia State University, 1980.
Campbell, D. *If I'm in charge here why is everybody laughing?* Allen, TX: Argus Communications, 1980.
Cooper, S. & Heenan, C. *Preparing, designing & leading workshops: A humanistic approach.* Boston, MA: CBI Pub. Co., Inc., 1980.
Cornell, A. H. *The decision-maker's handbook.* Englewood Cliffs, NJ: Prentice-Hall, 1980.
Dauw, D. C. *Creativity and innovation in organizations,* 4th ed. Prospect Heights, IL: Waveland Press, Inc., 1980.
Doyle, M. & Straus, D. *How to Make meetings work.* New York: Playboy Paperbacks, 1976.
Dyer, W. G. *Insight to impact: Strategies for interpersonal and organizational change,* Provo, UT: Brigham Young University Press, 1976.
Egan, G. *You and me: The skills of communicating and relating to others,* Monterey, CA: Brooks/Cole Publishing, 1977.
Ekvall, G. *Creativity at the place of work.* Stockholm: Swedish Council for Personnel Administration, 1971.
Engel, H. M. *Handbook of creative learning exercises.* Houston, TX: Gulf Publishing Co., 1973.
Fiedler, F. E. *Improving leadership effectiveness.* New York: Wiley, 1976.
Fluegelman, A. *The new games book.* San Francisco, CA: Headlands Press, Inc., 1976.
Fluegelman, A. *More new games!* Garden City, NY: Dolphin Books/Doubleday & Co., 1981.
Gazda, G. M. & Ashbury, F. R. *Human relations development.* Boston, MA: Allyn and Bacon, 1977.
Gordon, T. *Leader Effectiveness training (L.E.T.).* New York: Wyden Books, 1977.
Gryskiewicz, S. S. & Shields, J. T. (eds.) *The proceedings creativity week (1-5).* Greensboro, NC: Center for Creative Leadership, 1979-1983.
Gryskiewicz, S. S., Shields, J. T. & Sensabaugh, S. J. *Blueprint for innovation: Creativity week VI, 1983.* Greensboro, NC: Center for Creative Leadership, 1984.
Guthrie, E. & Miller, W. A. *Making change: A guide to effectiveness in groups.* Minneapolis, MN: Interpersonal Communication Programs, Inc., 1978.
Hanson, P. G. *Learning through groups: A trainer's basic guide.* San Diego, CA: University Associates, 1981.
Hare, A. P. *Creativity in small groups.* Beverly Hills, CA: SAGE, 1982.
Hare, A. P. *Handbook of small group research.* 2nd ed. New York: Free Press, 1976.
Harvard business review - On human relations (eds.). New York: Harper & Row, 1979.
Hersey, P. & Stinson, J. (eds.). *Perspectives in leader effectiveness.* Athens, OH: The Center for Leadership Studies, Ohio University, 1980.
Hersey, P. & Blanchard, K. *Management of organizational behavior: Utilizing human resources.* 4th ed. Englewood Cliffs, NJ: Prentice-Hall, 1982.
Horn, R. E. & Cleaves, A. *The guide to simulations/games for education and training,* 4th ed. Beverly Hills, CA: SAGE, 1980.
Hunsaker, P. & Allessandra, A. *The art of managing people.* Englewood Cliffs, NJ: Prentice-Hall, 1980.
Hunt, J. G. & Larson, L. L. *Leadership: The cutting edge.* Carbondale: Southern Illinois University Press, 1977.
Hunt, J. G. & Larson, L. L. *Crosscurrents in leadership.* Carbondale: Southern Illinois University Press, 1979.
Hyman, R. T. *Improving discussion leadership.* New York: Teachers College Press/Columbia University, 1980.
Johnson, D. W. & Frank P. *Joining together: group theory and group skills.* Englewood Cliffs, NJ: Prentice-Hall, 1975.
Jones, P. G. (ed.) *Adult learning in your classroom: The best in Training Magazine's strategies and techniques for managers and trainers.* Minneapolis, MN: Lakewood Publications, 1982.
Kanter, R. *The change masters: Innovation for productivity in the American corporation.* New York: Simon and Shuster, 1983.
Kaufman, R. *Identifying and solving problems: A systems approach,* 3rd ed. San Diego, CA: University Associates, 1982.
Koberg, D. & Bagnall, J. *The universal traveler.* Los Altos, CA: William Kaufmann, Inc., 1974.
Lassey, W. R. & Fernandez, R. R. (eds.) *Leadership and social change,* 2nd ed., San Diego, CA: University Associates, 1976.
Lawson, J. D., Griffin, L. J., & Donant, F. D. *Leadership is everybody's business: A practical guide for volunteer membership groups.* San Luis Obispo, CA: Impact Publishers, 1976.
Lawson, L. G., Donant, F. D., & Lawson, J. D. *Lead on! The complete handbook for group leaders.* San Luis Obispo, CA: Impact Publishers, 1982.
Locke, E. & Latham, G. *Goal setting: A motivational technique that works.* Englewood Cliffs, NJ: Prentice-Hall, 1984.
Lundstedt, S. & Colglazier, E. *Managing innovation.* New York: Pergamon Press, 1982.
Maier, N. R. F. *Problem solving and creativity: In individuals and groups.* Belmont, CA: Brooks/Cole Publishing Co., 1970.
McCall, M. W. Jr. & Lombardo, M. M. *Leadership: Where else can we go?* Durham, NC: Duke University Press, 1978.
Miner, J. B. *Theories of organizational behavior.* Hinsdale, IL: The Dryden Press, 1980.
Mouton, J. & Blake, R. *Synergogy: A new strategy for education, training and development.* San Francisco, CA: Jossey-Bass, 1984.

Nierenberg, G. I. *The art of creative thinking.* New York: Simon and Schuster, 1982.
Pfeifer, J. W. & Jones, J. *The annual handbook for group facilitators (1972-81).* San Diego, CA: University Associates.
Pfeifer, J. W. & Goodstein, L. D. *The (1982, 1983, 1984) annual for facilitators, trainers, and consultants.* San Diego, CA: University Associates.
Pollock, T. *Managing creatively: A practical guide to managing yourself and others.* Boston, MA: CBI Publishing Co., 1982.
Raudsepp, E. & Yeager, J. *How to sell new ideas: Your company's and your own.* Englewood Cliffs, NJ: Prentice-Hall, 1981.
Rogers, C. *Freedom to learn.* Columbus, OH: Charles E. Merrill Publishing Co., 1979.
Rogers, E. M. *Diffusion of innovations.* 3rd ed. New York: Free Press, 1983.
Rothberg, R. R. (ed.). *Corporate strategy and product innovation.* 2nd ed. New York: Free Press, 1981.
Ruben, B. D. & Budd, R. W. *Human communication handbook: Simulations and games, volume 1.* Rochelle Park, NJ: Hayden Book Co., Inc., 1975.
Simon, S. *Negative criticism.* Niles, IL: Argus Communications, 1978.
Steiner, G. *Strategic planning: What every manager must know.* New York: Free Press, 1979.
Swap, W. (ed.). *Group decision making.* Beverly Hills, CA: SAGE, 1984.
Tropman, J. *Effective meetings: Improving group decision-making.* Beverly Hills, CA: SAGE, 1980.
Van Gundy, A. *Managing group creativity: A modular approach to problem solving.* New York: American Management Assoc., 1984.
Von Oech, R. *A whack on the side of the head: How to unlock your mind for innovation.* Menlo Park, CA: Creative Thinking, 1982.
Watzlawick, P., Weakland, J. H. & Fisch, R. *Change: Principles of problem formulation and problem resolution.* New York: Norton, 1974.
Weinstein, M. & Goodman, J. *Playfair.* San Luis Obispo, CA: Impact Publishers, 1980.
Wexley, K. N. *Organizational behavior and personnel psychology.* Homewood, IL: Richard D. Irwin, Inc., 1977.
Yukl, G. A. *Leadership in organizations.* Englewood Cliffs, NJ: Prentice-Hall, 1981.
Zander, A. F. *Making groups effective.* San Francisco, CA: Jossey-Bass, 1982.

E. Bibliographies on Creativity:

Razik, T. *Creativity studies and related areas.* Buffalo, NY: Creative Education Foundation, 1965.
Rothenberg, A. & Greenberg, B. *The index of scientific writings on creativity: creative men and women.* Hamden, CT: Archon Books, 1974.
Roweton, W. *Creativity: a review of theory and research.* Occasional Paper Number Seven. Buffalo, NY: Creative Education Foundation, 197 .
Stievater, S. "Books on creativity and problem solving" in Parnes, S., Noller, R. and Biondi, A. *Guide to creative action.* New York: Charles Scribner's Sons, 1977. pp 288-314.

Media

In addition to books, articles, theses, and dissertations on creativity, there are also many tapes, films, filmstrips, instructional programs, and other resources which you may find helpful. The following sources will provide specific information about many media resources related to creativity.

Besemer, S. Media monitor: creative connections. *Curriculum Review,* 1983, *22(1),* 12-14.
Goldberg, M. Some 175 films on creativity. In: Parnes, S. J., Noller, R. B. & Biondi, A. M. (Eds.). *Guide to creative action.* New York: Charles Scribners Sons, 1977, 260-269.
Treffinger, D. J. Methods, techniques, and educational programs for stimulating creativity: 1982 revision. In: Tannenbaum, A. J. *Gifted children: psychological and educational perspectives.* New York: Macmillan, 1983, 467-504.
Williams, F. E. *Media for developing creative thinking in young children.* Buffalo, NY: Creative Education Foundation, 1968.

Training

There are several ways you can pursue additional training in the CPS approach that you've learned in this book. These include

- *Center for Creative Leadership*
  5000 Laurinda Drive
  P. O. Box P-1
  Greensboro, NC 27402-1660

The *Center* offers many programs and services to improve the practice of management in organizations, and conducts many research and training programs on leadership and innovation. A workshop on "Targeted Innovation" stresses application of creative problem-solving tools to real problems, especially in business, industry, and organizational leadership.

- *Center for Creative Learning*
  P. O. Box 619
  Honeoye, NY 14471-0619

The *Center* provides advanced training for individuals or small groups throughout the year, and also offers scheduled one-day, weekend, and week long workshops and seminars on CPS, thinking skills, leadership; CPS facilitation, and other related topics. Graduate credit is available as an option.

- *Creative Education Foundation*
  1050 Union Road
  Buffalo, NY 14224

The *Foundation* sponsors the *Annual Creative Problem-Solving Institute,* a week-long "celebration" of CPS learning opportunities each June in Buffalo, New York. *CPSI* brings together during this week more than 500 participants from many countries. The *Foundation* also offers other smaller, regional programs on an occasional basis.

- *Center for Studies in Creativity*
  State University College at Buffalo
  Chase Hall, 1300 Elmwood Avenue
  Buffalo, NY 14222-1095

This *Center* offers undergraduate courses in Creative Studies (which can lead to a Creative Studies Minor for students in any major), and a unique graduate program leading to a Master of Science degree in Creative Studies. The staff of the Center provides workshops, inservice and outreach activities, as well as research and information on creativity and innovation.

Related Materials

- **Workbook For Creative Problem Solving**
  Scott G. Isaksen & Donald J. Treffinger (ISBN 0-943456-11-8)

  A 28 page book containing a sampling of CPS methods and techniques used to develop and strengthen an individual's personal creative problem-solving abilities. The material is based on research and development conducted over a period of more than three decades.

- **Creative Problem-Solving Student Workbook**
  Scott G. Isaksen, Donald J. Treffinger & Patricia McEwen
  (ISBN 0-943456-12-6)

  A 16 page booklet designed and adapted for use with elementary and special education students. Field tested by the authors.

- Posters keyed to **Creative Problem Solving: The Basic Course**
  Scott G. Isaksen & Donald J. Treffinger

  Series of 5 large 17 x 22 posters, printed on heavy stock, keyed to major points presented in **Creative Problem Solving: The Basic Course.** Ideal visual aids for classroom or business presentations.

Prices and additional information on other materials in the areas of creativity, innovation, problem-solving, entrepreneurship, mentoring, leadership, intuition, dreams, education, business, and psychology are available upon request.

BEARLY LIMITED
149 York Street
Buffalo, New York 14213